A 2 Z

AND MORE SIGNS

edited by Julian Rothenstein   texts by Mel Gooding

 **Thames & Hudson**

Research and design: Julian Rothenstein
Consultant: Lutz Becker

Artwork: Terence Smiyan, Tom Trinkle   Production: Tim Chester

First published in the United Kingdom in 2006 by
Thames & Hudson Ltd, 181A High Holborn, London WC1V 7QX
www.thamesandhudson.com

Compilation © Redstone Press 2006

Introduction and texts © Mel Gooding 2003

British Library Cataloguing-in-Publication Data
A catalogue record for this book is available from the British Library

ISBN-13: 978-0-500-28604-3
ISBN-10: 0-500- 28604-3

Printed and bound by South Sea International Press, Hong Kong

Grateful acknowledgment is made to the following:

Merrill C. Berman, Jim Frank, The Merrill C. Berman Collection, New York / PhDr Iva Janáková, PhDr Koenigsmarkova, Alena Zapletalová, The Museum of Decorative Arts, Prague / Kerstin Hinkel, Norbert Kaut, Gutenberg-Museum, Mainz / Dr Stefan Soltek, Martina Weisz, Klingspoor Museum, Offenbach / Bertram Schmidt-Friderichs, Brigitte Raab, Verlag Hermann Schmidt, Mainz / Nigel Roache, Denise Roughan, St Bride's Printing Library, London / Pauline Rae, Jeremy Aynsley, The Royal College of Art, London / Martin Andrews, Department of Typography and Graphic Communication at The University of Reading, Middlesex David Batterham, David Batterham Rare Books, London / Xavier Bermúdez, Trama Visual, Mexico City / David Hillman, Sally Waterman. Pentagram, London / Wolfgang Hartmann, Fundación Tipografia Bauer, Barcelona / Walter R. Wybrands, BV Uitgeverij D Bataafsche Leeuw/Van Soeren & Co, Amsterdam / Neil Handley, British Optical Association Museum/ The College of Optometrists, London / Michael Collinge, Oliver Clark, Collinge & Clark, London / Jan Tholenaar, The Jan Tholenaar Collection, Amsterdam / Brian Webb, Trickett & Webb, London

Thanks also to: Hiang Kee, Richard Hollis, Alan Fletcher, David Wakefield, Jan Solpera, Misha Anikst, Marcela Ramirez, Piers Wardle, John L. Walters, Stanislav Kolibal, Marqueta Kolibal, Jan de Jong, Anne Clarke.

FEATURES:

introduction 7

the art of layout 25

optical eye charts 99

a czech modernist alphabet 163

sign-writer's alphabets 229

the antifascist schoolbook 291

captions 315

FIRST LETTER AND LAST WORD:
INTRODUCING A2Z

'With these twenty four soldiers of lead I will conquer the world.' (anonymous printer)

The letter, as an abstract written sign, developed from the pictogram, the simple drawing which accompanied speech into the making of the first human culture. The sign must exist, drawn by the finger in sand, marked in ash or ochre on the cave wall, scratched into clay by a stick, before the sound can be attached to it. 'All letters began as signs', wrote Victor Hugo, 'and all signs began as images.' In a famous and not entirely fanciful little essay, the great novelist found in the modern alphabet everything from the image of man's simplest shelter to the portent of his destiny and the sign of God:

'A is the roof, the gable with its crossbeam, the arch; or it is two friends greeting, who embrace and shake hands; D is the human back; B is the D on the D, back on the back, the hump; C is the crescent, the moon; E is the foundations, the pillar, the console and the architrave, all architecture in a single letter; F is the gibbet; G is the french horn; H is a façade with two towers; I is the war machine launching its projectile; J is the ploughshare and the horn of plenty; K is the angle of reflection equal to the angle of incidence, a key to geometry; L is the leg and foot; M is a mountain or a camp with tents pitched in pairs; N is a gate with a diagonal bar; O is the sun; P is a porter with a load on his back; Q is a rump with a tail; R is the porter resting on his staff; S is a serpent; T is a hammer; U is the urn, V the vase, which are easily confused; [Y is a tree, the fork of two roads, the confluence of two rivers, the head of a donkey or an ox, a stemmed glass, a lily on its stalk, a man praying with arms up-stretched]; X is crossed swords, a battle: who will win we do not know, so the mystics made it the sign of destiny and the algebraists the sign of the unknown; Z is lightning, the sign of God: ...that is what the alphabet contains.'

Of the making of alphabets there is no end, and this book has been made to illustrate that fact, and celebrate it. As the Celtic proverb has it, *every force evolves a form*: in human affairs necessity creates energies and out of energies evolve technologies. With the advent of printing - the defining technology of the modern world, the *sine qua non* of other modern technologies, perhaps the single most important invention since drawing - came the need for diverse letter forms to serve a multitude of functions. Every job demands the right typeface, the lettering that will serve its purposes best. So many alphabets for so many tasks in so many media: the stonemason's lapidary, the stencil-maker's schematic, the needleworker's stitchable, as well as the manifold forms that are necessary to the printer's trade proper. Each has a character and a feel of its own, each bears the imprint of its time and the marks of its *milieu*. Alphabets come in an infinite diversity: in some the letter forms are pure and simple, in others, complex, complicated, extravagant or fantastic. There are modest alphabets and flamboyant alphabets, silly alphabets and sad ones. Alphabets proliferate. In literate societies they are an index of human diversity: every child that learns to write invents its own, as distinctive as fingerprints. Every alphabet presents an orchestration of the letters to the eye, a systematic optical abstract, a visual matrix out of which any number of possible messages might be composed.

Not all alphabets are equal. Some are elegant, reflecting the grace and intelligence of their makers and users, fit for the transparent setting of subtle and beautiful language; some are workaday and simple, democratic in spirit, apt for plain writing, plain printing; others are squat and blocky, their ugly faces betraying the brutality of their time and place in history; others are ludic, capricious or idiosyncratic, drawing attention to their formal waywardness. Functional visual systems designed for communicative purposes, printed alphabets nevertheless speak for themselves and their time, assume recognisable style. They invite contemplation as free-standing artefacts of their culture, variously perfect, flawed, or simply queer. In every case they are *expressive*.

It is no contradiction of this fact that for many typographers and the printers and publishers they supply, especially those concerned with the setting of prose in books and newspapers, the perfect typeface is one in which the alphabet becomes invisible as the reader apprehends the matter carried by the complicated and rigorous arrangements of its individual characters. The set page is regarded by these perfectionists as a clear window upon meaning, every letterform balanced, every relation between letters in words, and between words in sentences, minimizing distraction from the message to the medium. 'Printing should be invisible' wrote Beatrice Warde, the writer and publicist for the Monotype Corporation in its golden years. For the redoubtable Stanley Morison, the doyen of typographers in that period, there was no room for argument: typography was 'the efficient means to an essentially utilitarian and only accidentally aesthetic end.... Therefore, any disposition of printing material which, whatever the intention, has the effect of coming between author and reader is wrong.'

For such typographers as Morison himself, Eric Gill, the American Bruce Rogers and the Dutchman Jan van Krimpen, revivalists of the great classic faces as well as inventors of elegant new functional ones, the letter must modestly and discreetly serve the text: 'If readers do not notice the consummate reticence and rare discipline of a new type it is probably a good letter', wrote Morison. Clarity and legibility were the watchwords of these militant traditionalists, and in England and the United States they carried all before them in the great typographical revival of the years between the wars.

The task of the type-designer, as they conceived it, was to achieve a balanced face, in which each letter would aspire to tonal equality with every other, and to a non-assertive unity of effect. The printer's job was to set the page with a symmetrical balance, vertically centring the text in such a way as to afford the least visual disturbance possible, and to ornament with taste and discretion only where the text allowed and the accepted aesthetic of the page would be positively served. There was an ethical purpose to this aesthetic: clarity of delivery enhanced communication; knowledge and argument conveyed with economy was essential to democratic understanding and thus to individual and collective freedom of thought.

These rigorous ideals, based on principles of public service in a spirit disposed to the democratic dissemination of knowledge and ideas, were advocated with a stolid eloquence in the writings of Morison, Gill, Paul Beujon, Rogers and others. They were exemplified with grace in beautifully produced publications such as, in England alone, Francis Meynell's *Typography* (1923), *The Fleuron* (seven issues from 1923 to 1932) and Oliver Simon's magazine *Signature* (first issue November 1935); and in a remarkable succession of printers' type-specimen books (notable among many others those issued by the Curwen Press 1928, Richard Clay & Sons 1930, the Kynoch Press 1934 and W.S. Cowell 1947). These latter contained complete alphabets set in every face used by the printer, in upper case, lower case, bold and italic, and in their various sizes, and frequently carried demonstration pages of text set and beautifully illustrated with original lithography.

Splendid as they might be, these specimen books were essentially commercial in intention, and they were limited, of course, to those type alphabets that the printers actually stocked and used in book, magazine and other kinds of printed production, cards, posters, handbills etc. It was, nevertheless, understood, from the early days of commercial printing in the seventeenth century, that the jobbing printer was necessarily at the heart of democratic communications, the essential journeyman (the daily worker!) in the cause of social change and reform, and printers were notable for their radical politics. In the *American Typefounders Manual* of 1941 some of the specimen pages were set with direct and eloquent statements of the democratic principles and functions of printing: 'Giving voice to the countless thousands who tell their story in the printed word is the function of type.' Other manuals on both sides of the Atlantic often contained wittily cryptic political messages. It should not surprise that one of the best typographical style books (manuals containing directions and advice on the styling of publications) of the post-war days of hope was Michael Middleton's *Soldiers of Lead*, issued by the Labour party in 1948, with an epigraph from *Areopagitica*, Milton's classic polemic against censorship of the printed word.

While the revivalists, high-minded and idealistic, but fundamentally conservative, were determining the new directions of book, magazine and newspaper design in this country and the USA, elsewhere, in Europe, things were different. In Russia, Germany and the Netherlands another kind of revolution in typography was taking place, inspired by the utopian ideals of Modernism, and led not only by letter designers and typographers but by major artists. In the pages of *De Stijl* and Kurt Schwitters's *Merz*, in the publications of the Bauhaus, in the work of El Lissitzky, László Moholy-Nagy, Herbert Bayer, H. N. Werkman and many others, a new and aggressively asymmetric typography was adopted, and advocated for universal use in the new age. To the *sans-serif* types of *die neue typographie* were accorded the attributes of an honest and unornamented beauty and clarity appropriate to the rational life of modern humankind.

The letter, freed from subordination to the word, leapt into visibility and proclaimed itself a concrete and independent component of the printed message. The settings of the message itself, poem or prose, information, advertisement or propaganda, aspired to the condition of the abstract image, dynamically entering the eye and the mind, challenging critical response, inviting action and reflection. A new style of photography, asymmetrical and emphasising the diagonal, was enlisted into the cause of communicative urgency, exemplified in different ways and in different moods in the work of such innovators as Alexander Rodchenko and André Kertész.

This collaboration with modernist art was based upon deep affinities. Behind these exciting developments in typography were the pioneering modernist abstractions of Kasimir Malevich, Piet Mondrian, Frantisek Kupka and Theo van Doesburg. 'There is a connection between modern typography and modern architecture' wrote Jan Tschichold, in his classic exposition *Asymmetrical Typography* (1935), 'but the new typography does not derive from the new architecture; rather both derive from the new painting, which has given to both a new significance of form…. [An abstract painting] is an instrument of spiritual power, a conception of harmony…. It is an appeal to order, a means to the improvement of mankind. It is not passive but dynamic.' The printed page was just such a mechanism, its energetic aesthetic having political and ethical purpose.

In France the stylish and *chic* dispositions of letter and motif of the more advanced journals and magazines of the modern period derived, typically, from home-grown artistic sources.

They were appropriated with Gallic *insouciance* from the graphic wit and vigour of Toulouse-Lautrec, from the jazzy *moderne* of *Art Deco*, first presented as such in 1925 at the Paris *Exposition Internationale des Arts Décoratifs et Industriels Modernes* of 1925, from the diverse variations of *mise-en-page* in the great *livres d'artistes*, and from the typographical poetic experiments of Mallarmé and Apollinaire. In the present volume this elegant eclectic stylism is especially celebrated in the pages from the Paris journal of printing design, *Arts et Métiers Graphiques*.

The letter is the point at which the structures of language meet the ground of the visible. It arrives in human culture long after speech in the order of things; long after the sounds uttered by humankind at its beginnings had separated into words, and these had been organised into systems of meaning. It was preceded in the world by visual signs, and has forever since been constantly accompanied by them. The visual sign, in its simple directness is the means by which the sounds of speech found their way towards the letter and the written word. In a book such as this, which presents the alphabet in many forms and many styles, and which is intended not only for practical use by designers, artists, poets and writers, but for the visual and intellectual pleasure of anyone who loves letters in their infinite variety, it is proper for the sign to be a vigorous and enlivening presence.

We live in an age in which the use of letters, and recourse to diverse alphabets, is unprecedented, and in which more alphabets have been invented than ever before in history. In the period of Modernism, to whose progressive and humane principles we pay homage in this book, there was access as never before to good design and visual diversity. In newspapers, magazines and books, on book jackets and film posters, in the packaging of objects and the advertisement of goods and services, on buildings, hoardings, in streets and public buildings, in the underground and on the buses, wherever information was conveyed, there was evidence of the most intelligent and aesthetically sophisticated combination of utility and beauty.

In this book, for example, there is reproduced a series of sign-writers' alphabets intended to find their public realisation on shop fronts and bar signs; there are elegant eye charts for the optician's patient; there are letters and signs for technical manuals; there are fine typographies for beautiful books; there is a magisterial Constructivist alphabetic ballet; and so on. Every task demands its own kind of alphabet; every new purpose evolves its appropriate new lettering. This book is not like the many alphabet books and surveys that already exist, utilitarian collections of particular alphabets; neither is it a type-specimen book, or a manual of style and layout. It has no programme, and it has no system of presentation, confuses categories and obeys no rules. It reflects, rather, the taste and interest of the editors, their affection for the wayward as well as for the rigorous in matters of design and typography, their love for all manner of lettering, typography and sign-making. It delights in the multifarious printed signs that jostle 'the visible word' and make a mark on the visual world – in fleurons and flourishes, decorations and clichés, vignettes, trademarks, logos. It is a book made for all lovers of letters and signs, for their use and for their delight.

MEL GOODING NOVEMBER 2005

Note: this Introduction is adapted and expanded from the introductory texts to *Alphabets and Other Signs* and *ABZ: More Alphabets and other Signs* (Redstone Press, London 1991 and 2004 respectively)

ARTS ET MÉTIERS GRAPHIQUES

AM
G
61

FREGIO MECANO

(Carattere scomponibile)

Minimo Kg. 2,50   Si vendono anche figure separate : minimo Kg. 1 per figura

Le poème électronique se propose
de montrer au sein d'un tumulte
angoissant notre civilisation partie
à la conquête des temps modernes.
LE CORBUSIER.

Cette suite de planches ne saurait être la reproduction du
Poème Electronique, celui-ci étant un ensemble de sons, de
lumière, d'images, de rythme et de couleur, abrité dans une
architecture, volume spécifiquement dépendant de l'espace.
Cette réalisation graphique n'est qu'une interprétation uti-
lisant quelques uns des documents choisis par Le Corbusier.

harmonie

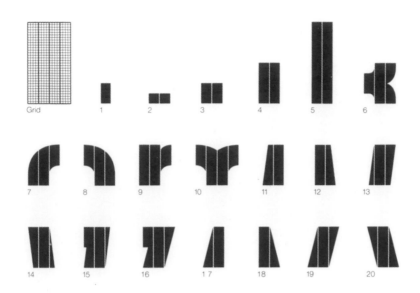

Grid 1 2 3 4 5 6

7 8 9 10 11 12 13

14 15 16 17 18 19 20

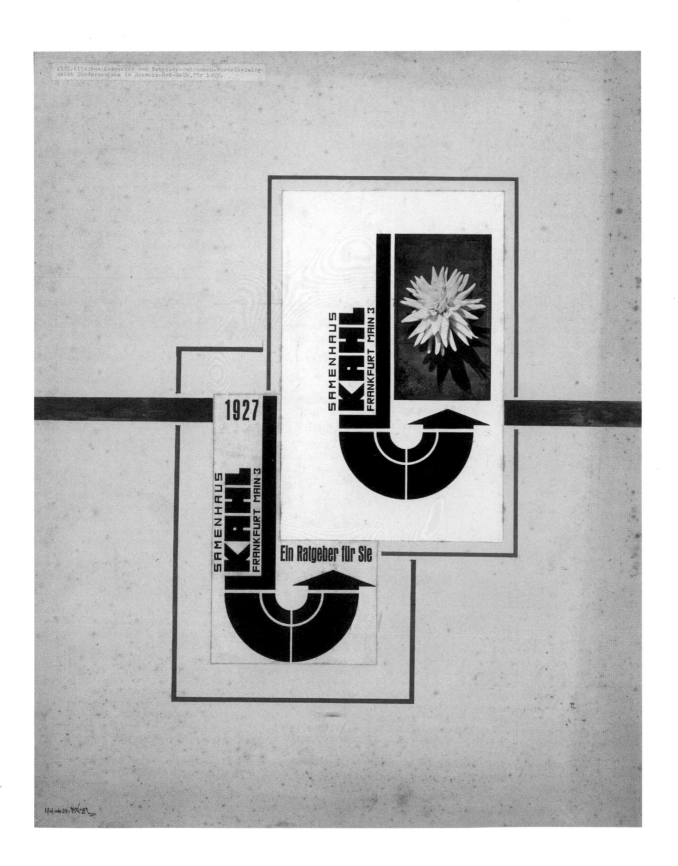

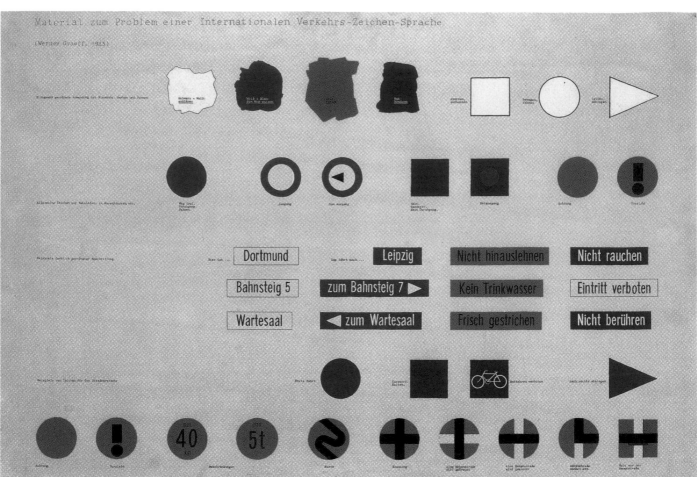

Material zum Problem einer Internationalen Verkehrs-Zeichen-Sprache

(Werner Graeff, 1923)

Dortmund

Bahnsteig 5

Wartesaal

Leipzig

zum Bahnsteig 7 ▶

◀ zum Wartesaal

Nicht hinauslehnen

Kein Trinkwasser

Frisch gestrichen

Nicht rauchen

Eintritt verboten

Nicht berühren

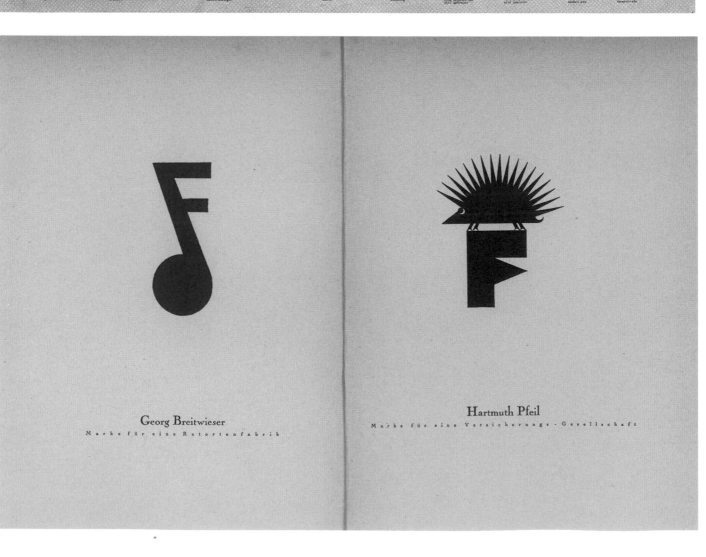

Georg Breitwieser
Marke für eine Retortenfabrik

Hartmuth Pfeil
Marke für eine Versicherungs-Gesellschaft

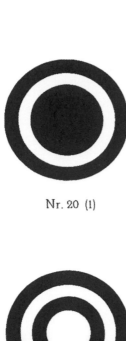

Nr. 20 (1)

Nr. 25 (4)

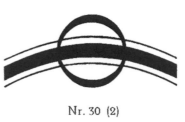

Nr. 30 (2)

Nr. 21 (1)

Nr. 26 (2)

Nr. 31 (2)

Nr. 22 (1)

Nr. 27 (2)

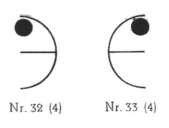

Nr. 32 (4)   Nr. 33 (4)

Nr. 34 (4)

Nr. 23 (1)

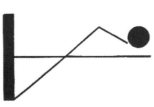

Nr. 28 (2)

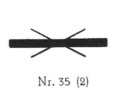

Nr. 35 (2)

Nr. 24 (2)

Nr. 29 (2)

Nr. 36   Nr. 37   Nr. 38

Einfassung 1 m

L'AUTOMOBILE

ETOILE DE

L'INDUSTRIE FRANÇAISE

Tous les drapeaux du monde sont faits en soie de Lyon

le témoin.

DIRECTEUR PAUL IRIBE N° 63 19 MAI 1935 LE N° UN FRANC

LA LOTERIE

A TOUS LES COUPS L'ON PERD

GAIETE SAGESSE
Loyauté
FRANÇAISES

The art of lay-out nowadays owes its strength to its free use of processes. From photographic apparatus, scissors, a bottle of Indian ink, a gumpot, combined with the hand of the designer and an unprejudiced eye, a composition can be evolved and a novel idea expressed by simple means.

SILENCE

THE ART OF LAYOUT

Mise en Page: The Theory and Practice of Lay-out, by A. Tolmer, was published by *The Studio* magazine in 1932. The genius of the booklet was to instruct by example, and its texts were models of modernist economy and grace. The virtues it sought to inculcate were those of simplicity, balance, clarity of expression, and freedom from preconceptions on the use of materials and processes. Apart from its exemplary value as a design manual what gives *Mise en Page* an undeniable poignancy is the conviction it professes, in text and design, in the necessity to civilised life of principled thought and humane feeling in good practice. For Tolmer, as for Wittgenstein, it seems, "ethics and aesthetic are one".

PREFACE

ike skating or walking the tight-rope, the art of lay-out is an art of balance.

t cannot however be expressed merely as a mathematical calculation. The tight-rope walker steadies herself with her parasol rather than with the aid of a formula. The sense of stability; the right and the wrong way of doing anything; the amount of air that enables the earth to breathe; the amount of sleep that permits of the greatest activity during the day; the most satisfactory way of combining the elements of a theatre-set, the page of a book or a poster; all these things are essentially a matter of feeling.

he feelings of mankind are unaffected by the change of ideas, constructive and destructive by turns, which accompany each phase of history. Since the earliest times known to us, love, hate, joy, suffering and religion have exercised a constant influence. Every age and every civilization, therefore, must be guided by these basic impulses and the works produced under their influence, in order to test, control, and correct its own balance.

So, considering the past, we might have written simply an historical study of the kind of balance represented by the art of lay-out. But this we have wished to avoid. If an historical evolution may be traced in the series of illustrations here reproduced it will not be by any means complete.

An investigation has been made into the origins of the art of lay-out. The part played by the shape of text in a lay-out has been demonstrated by reference to various types of ancient writing. The links between letterpress, ornament, and architecture have been pointed out. Points of comparison between modes of lay-out used in different countries and at different periods have been established. The sole aim, however, has been that of providing rich materials for the modern method of approach.

It is always a difficult matter for the professional tennis-player to discuss his game. But this is not a series of lessons in lay-out. We wish to immerse our readers in the subject and to prime them with information which will enable them to infuse fresh life and a continually changing novelty into their practice of it.

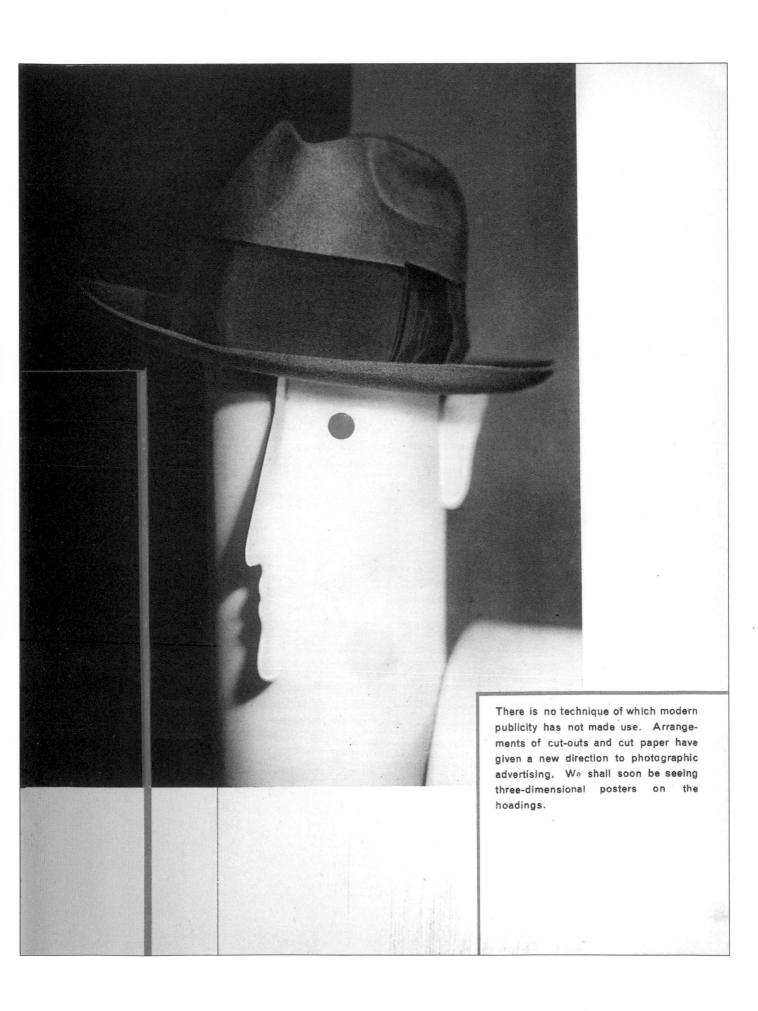

There is no technique of which modern publicity has not made use. Arrangements of cut-outs and cut paper have given a new direction to photographic advertising. We shall soon be seeing three-dimensional posters on the hoadings.

Photography gives concrete form to the subtlest thoughts. It has the gift of imparting to the dullest, most mechanical and impersonal things the sensitiveness and poetry which admits them into our dreams.

R. MANIFATTURA TABACCHI · ROVIGNO D'ISTRIA

RIVISTA DI ESTETICA E TECNICA GRAFICA MENSILE ANNO VII N. 3-5 MARZO-MAGGIO 1939 XVII SPEDIZIONE IN ABBONAMENTO POSTALE

CAMPO GRAFICO
AEROPORTO DELLA
RIVOLUZIONE
FUTURISTA DEL·
LE PAROLE IN LI
BERTÀ POESIA
PUBBLICITARIA

italiana velocità simultaneità

F.T. Marinetti

EXCELSIOR ZWICKY

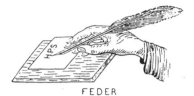

FEDER

AU CYGNE

H K

SOLTEX ZEGNA

PASTA SPECIALE AL PURO UOVO

"la Perfetta"

INDUSTRIA PASTE ALIMENTARI
CAV. LUIGI SESTI
LUCCA Italy

STAGI CORTI & C LIVORNO

EXCELSIOR ZWICKY

ARBEITE, SAMMLE, VERMEHRE.

MARQUE DÉPOSÉE

DEGEA

PASTA SPECIALE AL PURO UOVO

OLYMPIA

MARCA DEPOS

FABBRICATO DA
S.A.BORGHI-MILANO

AÑO IV - NUMERO 3 (20)   MAYO - JUNIO 1953

SIN⊖SIS

R E V I S T A   M E D I C A
EDITADA POR ''ESTABLECIMIENTOS MEXICANOS COLLIERE, S. A.''

ATAVIOS DE LOS DIOSES.—*Códice matritense del Real Palacio.*

ARTE PREHISPANICO por *Vladimiro Rosado Ojeda, pág. 19*

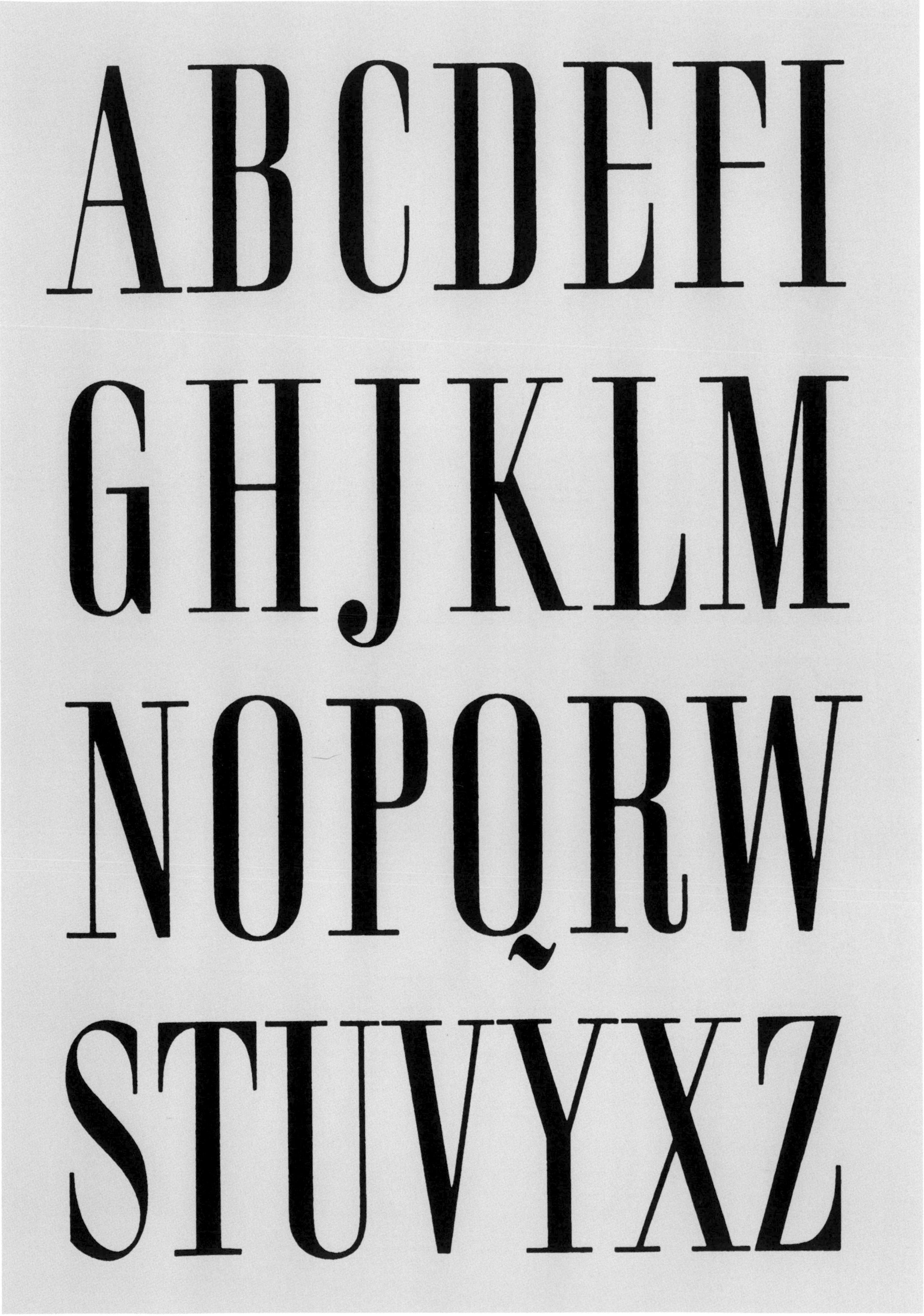

ABCDEFI
GHJKLM
NOPQRW
STUVYXZ

abcdefg
hijklno
mpqrfw
stuvxyz

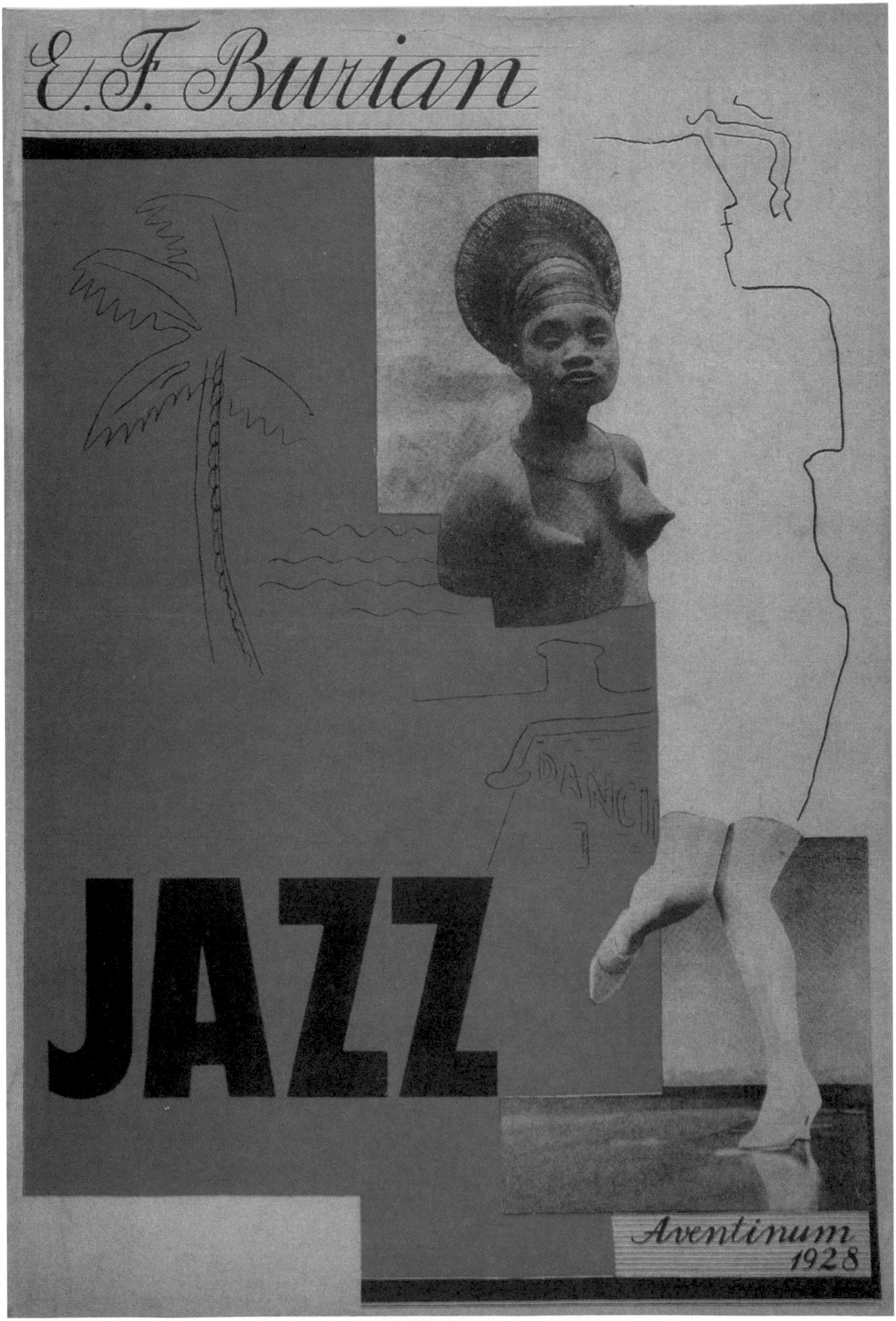
E.F. Burian
DANCI
JAZZ
Aventinum
1928

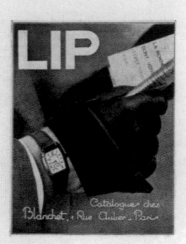

Publicité Dam.

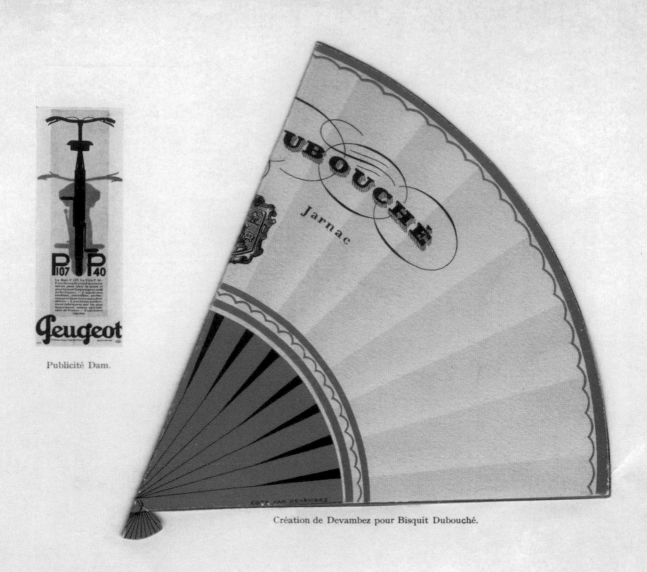

Création de Devambez pour Bisquit Dubouché.

Annonce pour les montres Lip.

Page d'annonce (Édit. Paul-Martial).

Dessin de Francis Bernard
(Édit. Paul-Martial).

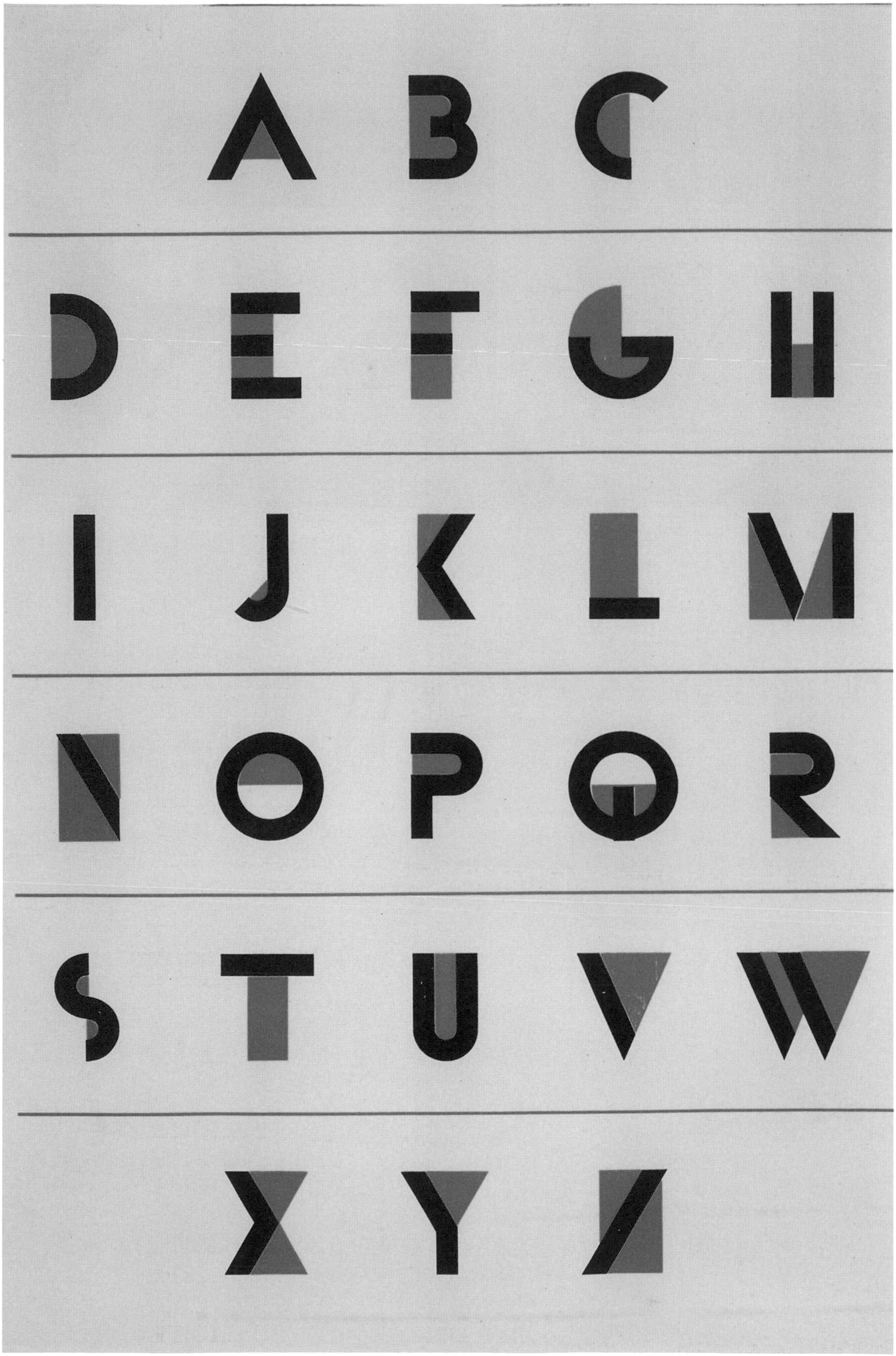

A B C

D E F G H

I J K L M

N O P Q R

S T U V W

X Y Z

ı ı ı ı u n m r c a o e w x z ž s j

y q g p l t d b h ch k f

I H L F E T J U C G O Q X Y V W ž Ž

I. II. V. X.   *A M N D P B R K S*   L. C. D. M.

1 2 3 4 5 6 7 8 9 0 .

Achilles, Tantalus, Palermo, Vesuv.

A B C Č D E F G H I J K L M N O P Q R
Ř S Š T U V W X Y Z Ž &
a b c d e f g h i j k l m n o p q r s t u v w x y z
1 2 3 4 5 6 7 8 9 0   I. II. III. IV. V. VI. VII. VIII. IX. X.

A B C Č D E F G H I J K L M N O P
Q R Ř S Š T U V W X Y Z Ž &
a b c d e f g h i j k l m n o p q r s t u v x y z
1 2 3 4 5 6 7 8 9 0   I. II. III. IV. V. VI. VII. VIII. IX. X.

OT. ŠTORCH-MARIEN

KILIMA-NDŽARO LÁSKY

ABCDEFGH
IJKLMNOP
QRSTUVXY
ZWÇÆŒ&

abcdefghij
klmnopqrs
tuvxyzwçæ
œ.,:;'-!?(),,

1234567890

ABCDE
FGHIJKLM
NOPQRST
UVXYZWÇ
ÆŒ&

abcdefghij
klmnopqrs
tuvxyzwç
æœ.,:;'-!?(),,

1234567890

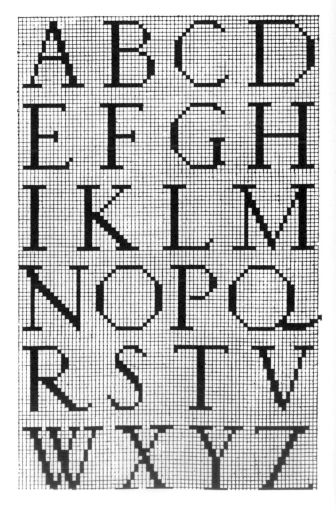

le mot.

N° 2. — 1re Année. **10 Centimes** **Lundi 7 Déc. 1914.**

LOHENGRIN ET L'ÉCREVISSE DESSIN DE PAUL IRIBE

LA MARCHE SUR PARIS.

TOME 1

TRAVAUX DE VILLE

CHAMBORD MAIGRE

ABCDEFGHIJK
LMNOPQR
STUVWXYZ

ÇÆŒÉÈËÊ&-?!()«»:';,.

abcdefghijklmn
opqrstuvwxyz

çæœàäâéèëêïîöôùüû

1234567890

COMPAGNONS DE COCAGNE

MENU POTAGE VELOUTÉ CAROLINE • ENDIVES AU JUS

DU 12 NOVEMBRE
CHEZ
VINCENT CANDRÉ
RUE SAINT ANDRÉ DES ARCS

TURBOT DE DIEPPE AU BEURRE D'ISIGNY • PERDREAUX

COQ A LA BERRICHONNE

VIN ROSÉ DE BOLÈNE

VIN BLANC DE POUILLY-SUR-LOIRE

PINOT DU SANCERROIS

CHAVIGNOLE

CAFÉ

FINE ET ARMAGNAC

HARICOTS VERTS

SALADE PANACHÉE
FROMAGES FLANQUÉS D'ALOUETTES

POMMES BONNE FEMME

CORBEILLE DE FRUITS

Menu du XVI° dîner des Compagnons de Cocagne

MARMITE NORMANDE. TURBAN D'ANGUILLE AU CHABLIS. SELLE DE VEAU FARCIE ORLOFF AVEC UNE GARNITURE PRINTANIÈRE. ASPERGES DE VINEUIL SAUCE HOLLANDAISE. CŒUR DE ROMAINE A L'HUILE D'OLIVE. FROMAGES. FRAISES CHANTILLY. CORBEILLE DE FRUITS. CAFÉ. EAUX-DE-VIE DU PAYS

MÂCON BLANC EN CARAFE. FLEURIE EN PICHET. GEVREY CHAMBERTIN

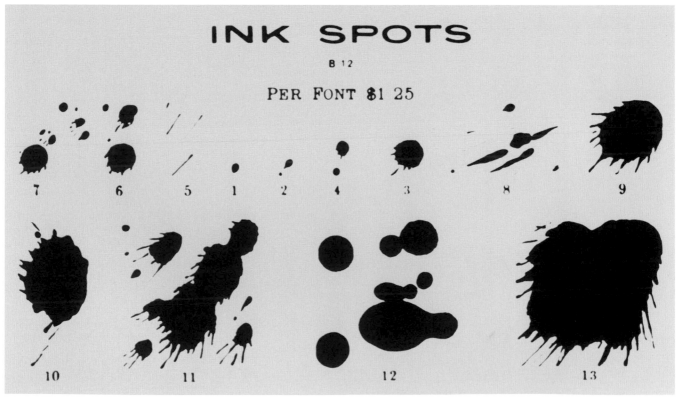

INK SPOTS

B 12

PER FONT $1 25

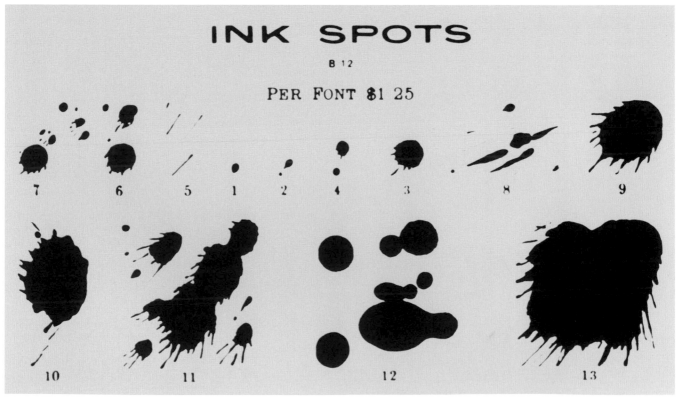

7 6 5 1 2 4 3 8 9

10 11 12 13

120 Point   3 A

CARDS WON

96 Point   3 A

RACKET PROBE

84 Point   3 A

EXCITING GAMES

72 Point   3 A

BOY FOUND MONEY

60 Point   4 A

BIG FIRE

Characters in Complete Font

ABCDEFG
HIJKLMN
OPQRST
UVWXYZ
& $1234
567890
.,-'':;!?

36 Point   8 A

HURRICANES

30 Point   8 A

LOVELY SPRING
COMING NORTH

48 Point   6 A

NEW KING

42 Point   7 A

HEADLINES

24 Point   12 A

SIGNING MEASURE
FIGHTS CHAMPION

51

त तरबूज

थ थरमस

द दवात

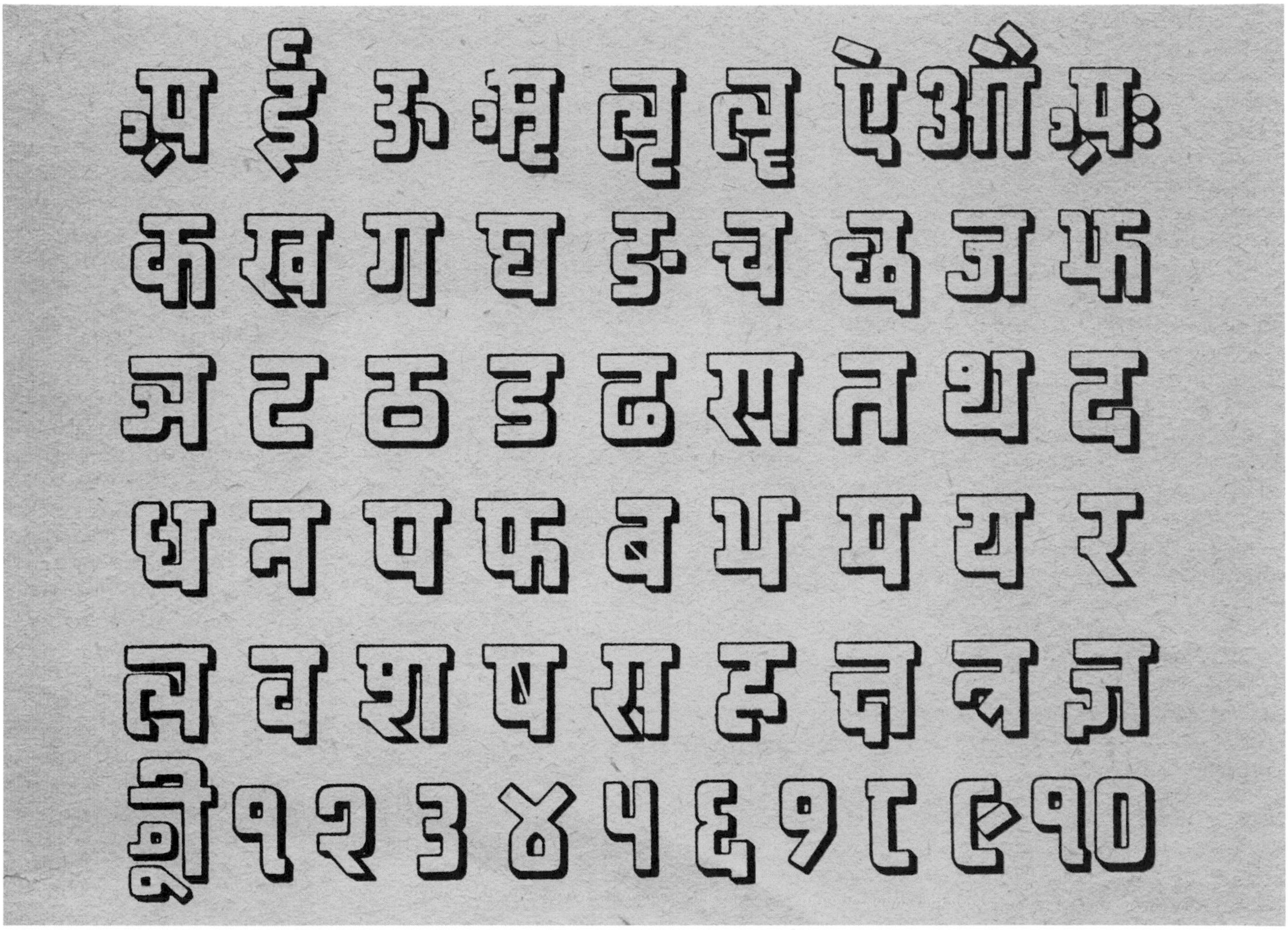

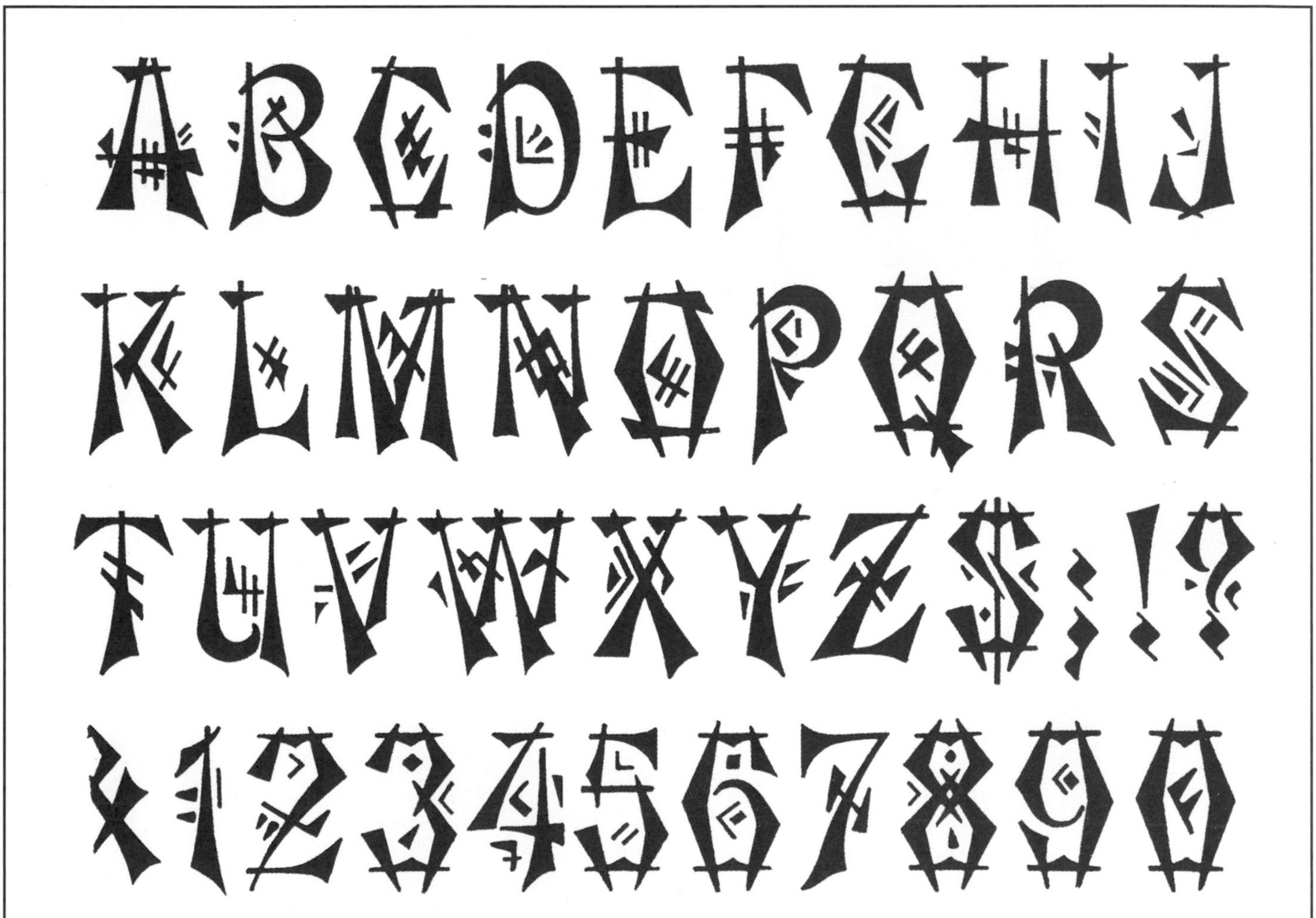
ABCDEFGHIJ
KLMNOPQRS
TUVWXYZ$;!?
1234567890

АБВГД
ЕХЗИЙ
КЛМНО
ПРСТУ
ФХЦЧШ
ЩЫЮЯ
Ь

К. ЭГГЕРТ

ТЕА-КИНО-ПЕЧАТЬ

abdeghk
npqe uu
mu dos
xyzfijrtl

SPECIMENS OF WOOD LETTER

MANUFACTURED BY

WRIGHT & CO.,

157, SOUTHWARK BRIDGE ROAD, LONDON, S.E.

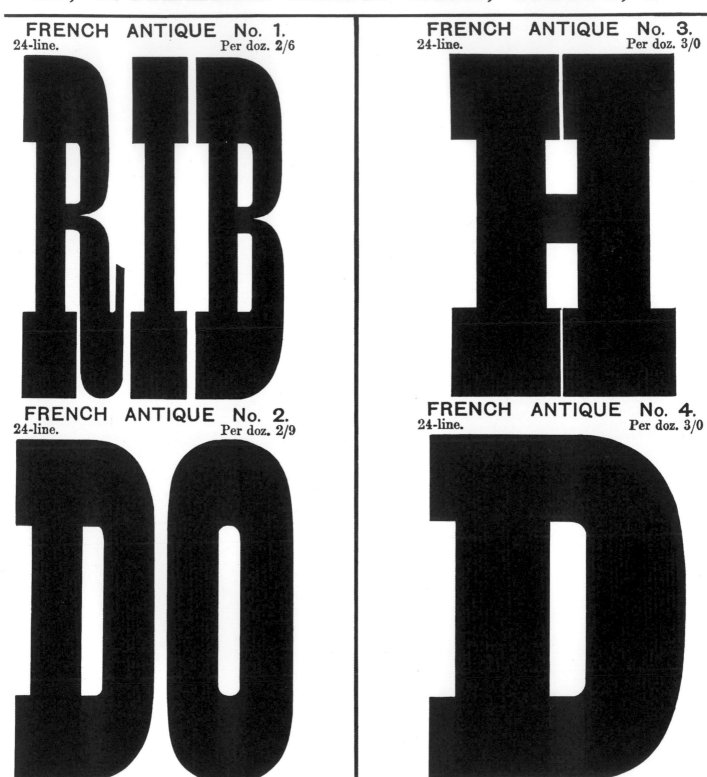

FRENCH ANTIQUE No. 1.
24-line.   Per doz. 2/6

FRENCH ANTIQUE No. 3.
24-line.   Per doz. 3/0

FRENCH ANTIQUE No. 2.
24-line.   Per doz. 2/9

FRENCH ANTIQUE No. 4.
24-line.   Per doz. 3/0

THESE LETTERS CAN BE CUT TO ANY SIZE AT PROPORTIONATE PRICES.

All the above can be supplied cut on Side Grain Box Wood or End Grain Maple at 25 % extra.

le témoin.

DIRECTEUR PAUL IRIBE   N° 6   14 JANVIER 1934   LE N° 1 FRANC 50

PRUDENCE
EST MÈRE DE LA SURETÉ

Specimens of Embossing
Waterlow Brothers & Layton, Limited,
24 & 25, Birchin Lane, London, E.C.

A B C D E F G H I
J K L M N O P Q R
S T U V W X Y Z &
a b c d e f g h i j k l m
n o p q r s t u v w x y z
1 2 3 4 5 6 7 8 9

THE MADRAS TYPE FOUNDRY, - - MADRAS-

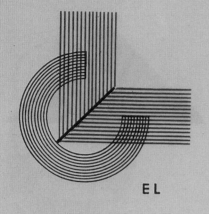

EL

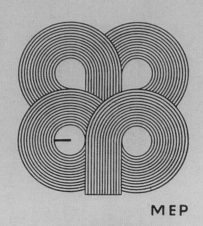

MEP

MA

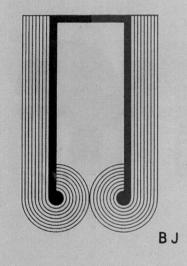

BJ

DT

SJ

MODÈLES DE

JEAN PUIFORCAT

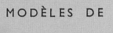

BC

SE

AP

ABCDEFGHIJKLM
NOPQR
STUVWXYZ

&ÇÆŒÉÈÊË-?!()""""«»:';,.

abcdefghijklmno
pqrstuvwxyz

çæœàäâéèëêïîöôûùü

1234567890

ABCD
EFGHI
KLMN
OPQR
STUV
WXYZ

„BERKEL" WEDSTRIJD 1 JAN.–30 JUNI 1928

HY

SLOEG HET HOOGST

A. BOTERMANS Jr.	141,3 %
J. C. KOOPMAN	141,- %
E. ROMEIJN	124,- %
D. DIJKSTRA	121,9 %
W. LEGERSTEE	121,6 %
G. DIEPENHEIM	118,2 %
J. REBEL	113,9 %
H. G. BOTERMANS	110,3 %
H. HENNINK	106,9 %
A. VAN VELZEN	102,1 %
A. NOORDHOFF	98,- %
M. DERKSEN	96,6 %
A. BAMMENS	94,7 %
C. VAN HOLST	92,9 %
W. DE HAAS	90,- %
F. GOOSEN	87,5 %
H. J. F. KIECKENS	82,3 %
D. VAN BELLE	82,5 %
A. VOGEL	80,1 %
D. VISSER	73,7 %
H. VAN BOSSUM Sr.	68,3 %

STAND OP 1 JUNI

RECLAME PAUL SCHUITEMA

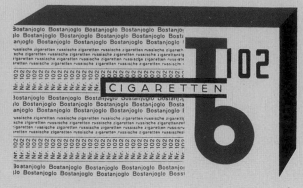

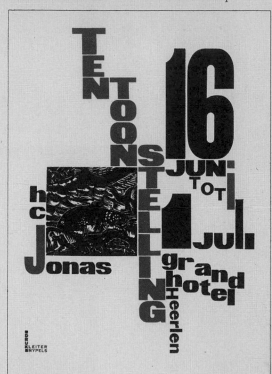

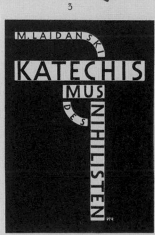

1, Franz Stautner, Mannheim. Geschäftskarte der Buchdruckerei G. Jacob, Mannheim. 2, Grete Stern, Stuttgart. Cigaretten-packung. 3, Buchdruckerei C. Nypels, Maastricht. Plakat für eine Kunstausstellung. 4, Erich Matthes, Erasmus-Druck, Berlin. Anzeige für MK-Papier. 5, 7, Nicolai Ilijin, Nishnij-Nowgorod. Zwei Buchumschläge. 6, Unbek. Buchumschlag

TYPOGRAPHISCHE BEISPIELE

ABCDEFGHIJ
KLMNOPQR
STUVWXYZ

abcd
efgh
ijkl
mno
pqrs
tuvw
xyz

HÁNOSŮĚBL
JDCKMPRW
ČVXZYŮIFT

nahebydskr
ctmfjópžgvl
wx2345678u

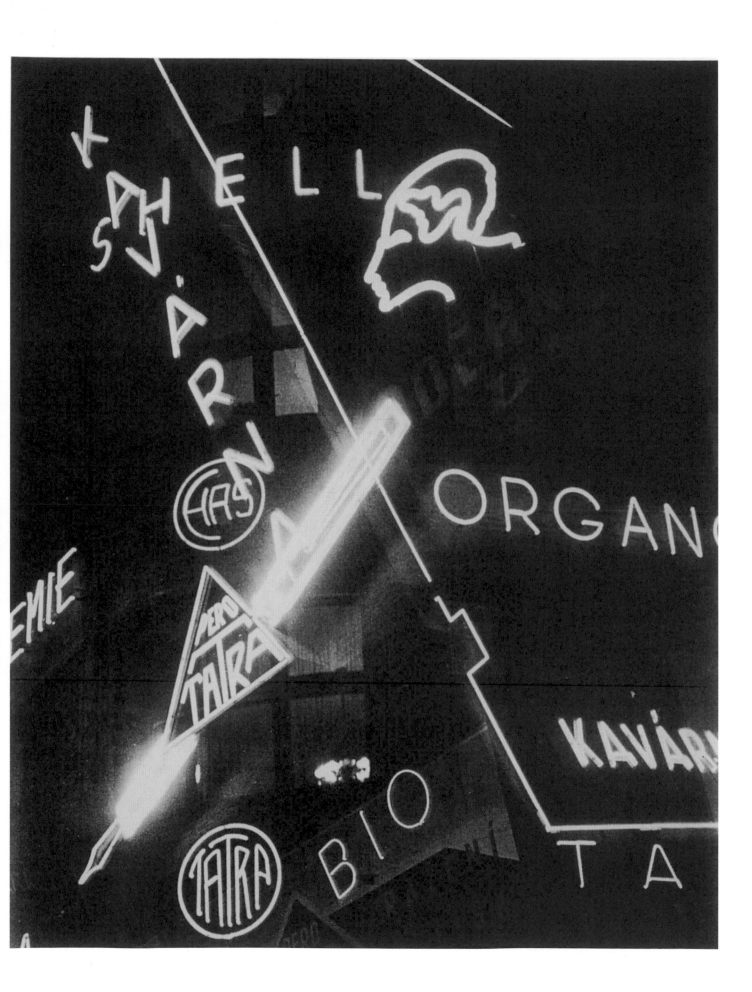

MUSTDIE

P P U

ANNIHILATOR

DEATH DUST

There are no flies on me.
I use "ANTIBUZZBUZZ."

"Antibuzzbuzz"

A1

FLY PREVENTIVE

NOTIX

WE ARE HERE TO-DAY

CLEAN
FATAL
NON-POISONOUS
LASTING

"SOLVENTO"

AND
GONE TO-MORROW

KWIKHEAL

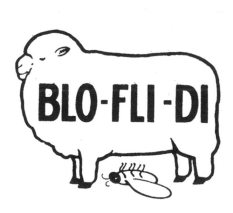

BLO-FLI-DI

PRODUCT OF EVERLASTING LABORATORIES

DETHBLO
The Insect Foe

GOT--U

Non-Poisonous Sanitary Fly-Paper

THE BUGS' FUNERAL
INSECSTERMINATOR

ABCDE
FGHIJ
KLMNO
PQRST
UVXYZ

ABCDEFGHIJ
KLMNOPQRS
TUVWXYZ&

Grecian XX Condensed. First shown by John Cooley in

LA MARQUE DE LA BÊTE

rlement, encore tout plein
de village. Paris, cœur de
t plus fortement l'accès de
France tout entière était

Remettons-nous dans c
tiple, houleux, comme un
qui jetait un peuple ent
chés du Palais-Bourbon.
deux partis à prendre :

SOCIETEIT voor CULTUREELE SAMENWERKING

EXCELSIOR THEATER
ZEESTRAAT
GASTVOORSTELLINGEN
DIE JUNGE TRUPPE
(BERLIN)

18 TOT 23 JANUARI 1931
DER ANDERE
VON MIGUEL DE UNAMUNO
DEUTSCH VON OTTO BUCK
DRAMA IN DREI AKTEN MIT EINEM EPILOG

DER ANDERE . . . . GILLIS VAN RAPPARD

LAURA . . . . ELLEN DAGMAR

DIAMIANA . . . . SYBIL RARES

ERNESTO. . . . . EMILIO CARGHER

AVITO . . . . HANS ALVA

DIE AMME. . . . . ERIKA KRISTEN

REGIE: GILLIS VAN RAPPARD

PRIJZEN DER PLAATSEN
ZAAL 1e DEEL FL. 3.00 ZAAL 2e DEEL FL. 2.50
ZAAL 3e DEEL EN BALCON FL. 1.25
PLAATSEN TE BESPREKEN DAGELIJKS
AAN HET GEBOUW VAN 10 TOT 16 UUR

VAN 24 TOT 31 JANUARI
DIE QUADRATUR DES KREISES
LUSTSPIEL VON VAL: KATAJEW

ONTWERP V. HUSZAR

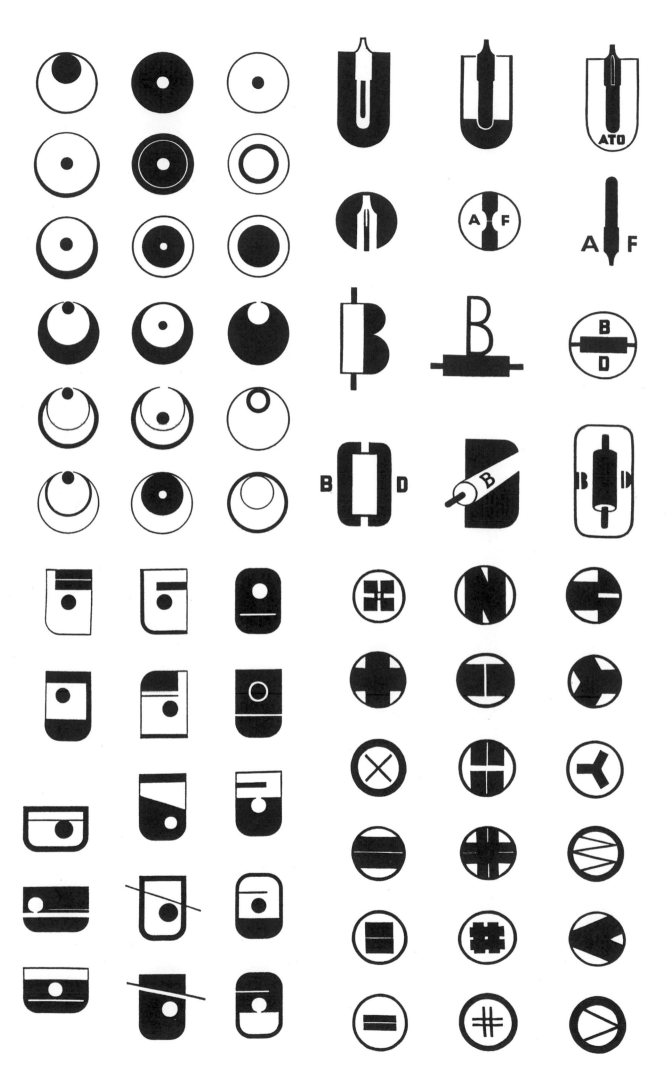

SOFFICI

** ⭐ .... ⭐⭐⭐

POESIA questo vertice dell'universo

FUTURIS

ANNO DELLA GUERRA 1914-1915

acerba

BÏFꟅZF+18

simultaneità e

TIPOGR
VALLECCHI
TELEFONO 23-91

IOR

haf pistpue famt a
famonit rusa pedia
F F sutnbm n
tubat menna tlie
o punmnvvrsn
alas resoso ap
stocchi amater
imatlis kaaa ne
sehi ap app smmt
atoteto halvi pise
naranaaa Rododomsi
imlaghroneasieuorp
Njou 22 nao vestit
IN maaee f = sem
stazzit
ra o ra

L. 5

Chimismi lirici

Firenze Edizioni della "Voce„

7 ДНЕЙ М.К.Т ДЕКАБРЬ

ЧЕЛОВЕК, КОТОРЫЙ БЫЛ ЧЕТВЕРГОМ.

1. Секретарь (понедельник) – С. Тихонравов.
2. Гоголь (вторник) – Н. Царский.
3. Проф. Борис (среда) – В. Соколов.
4. Сайм (четверг) – В. Поротиков.
5. Маркиз (пятница) – А. Фомин.
6. Докт. Буль (суббота) – С. Иович.
7. Председатель (воскресенье) – В. Артёмов.

N7

HNBDIČRMKÉ
GOPAVSYUWL
JSTZXFMYJQ!,
1234567890:
abrphxfcvdn,
stgmjuyeikz

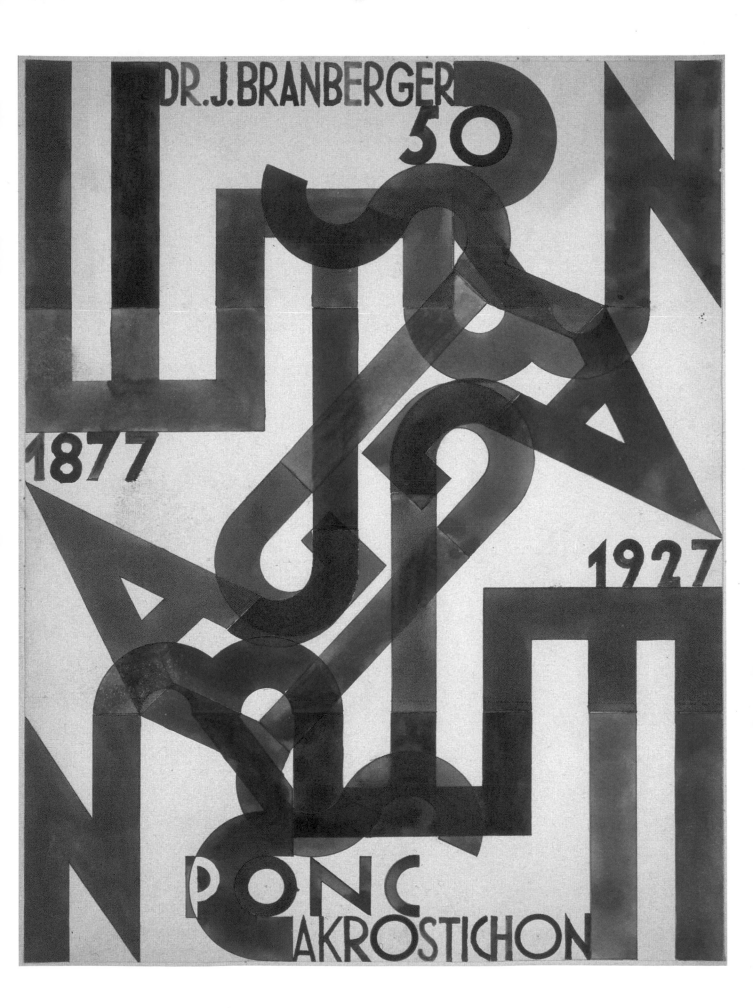

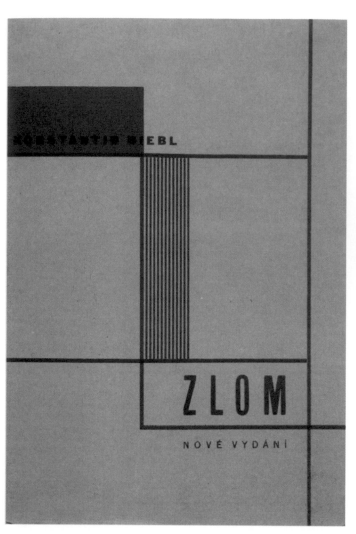

KONSTANTIN BIEBL

ZLOM

NOVÉ VYDÁNÍ

BÁSEŇ
NOCI 5.
SVAZEK
EDICE
OLYMP
PRAHA
1926

diabolo

Vítězslav Nezval

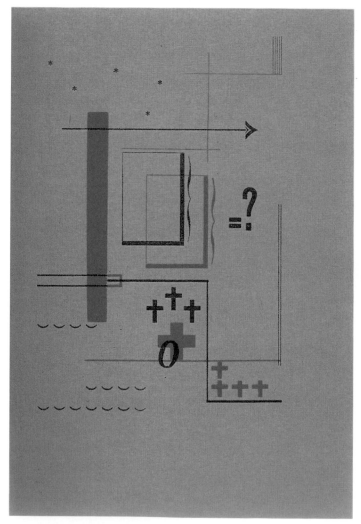

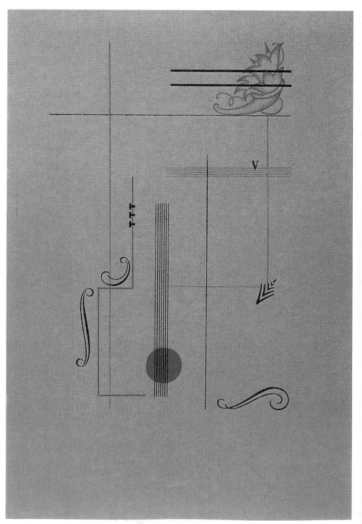

ABCDEFGHIJ
KĽMNOPQŘS
ŽĆŘTUVXYZW !?

АБВГГДЕДЖЗИЙК
ЛЛМНОПРСТУФХ
ЦЧШЩЪЭЮЯЯЁЬЫЪ

83

現在の特性と
未來の特性の
術

abcdefghij
klmnopqrs
tuvwxyz
1234567890

Cleverly stimulates the intricate, tangled appearance of Chinese writing. These letters would be picturesque for headline or initial use in suggesting Far Eastern atmosphere.

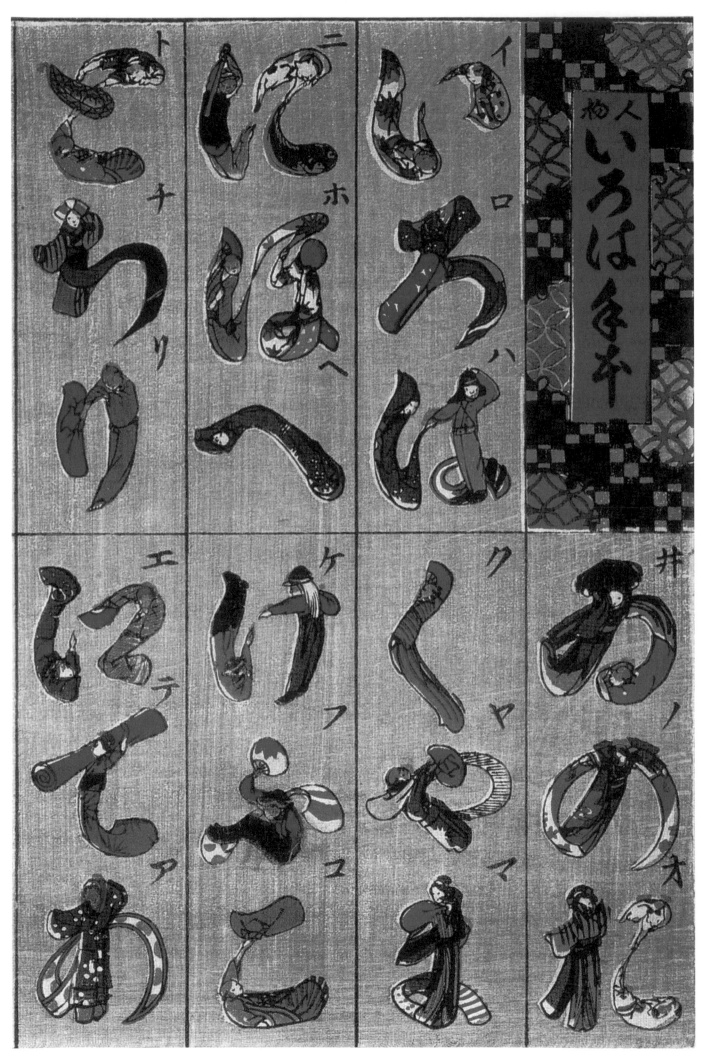

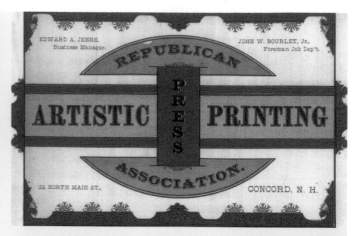

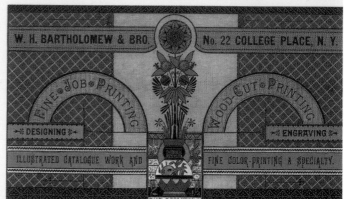

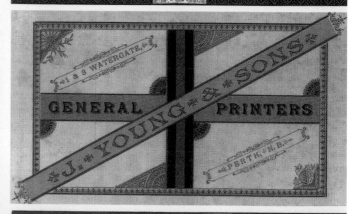

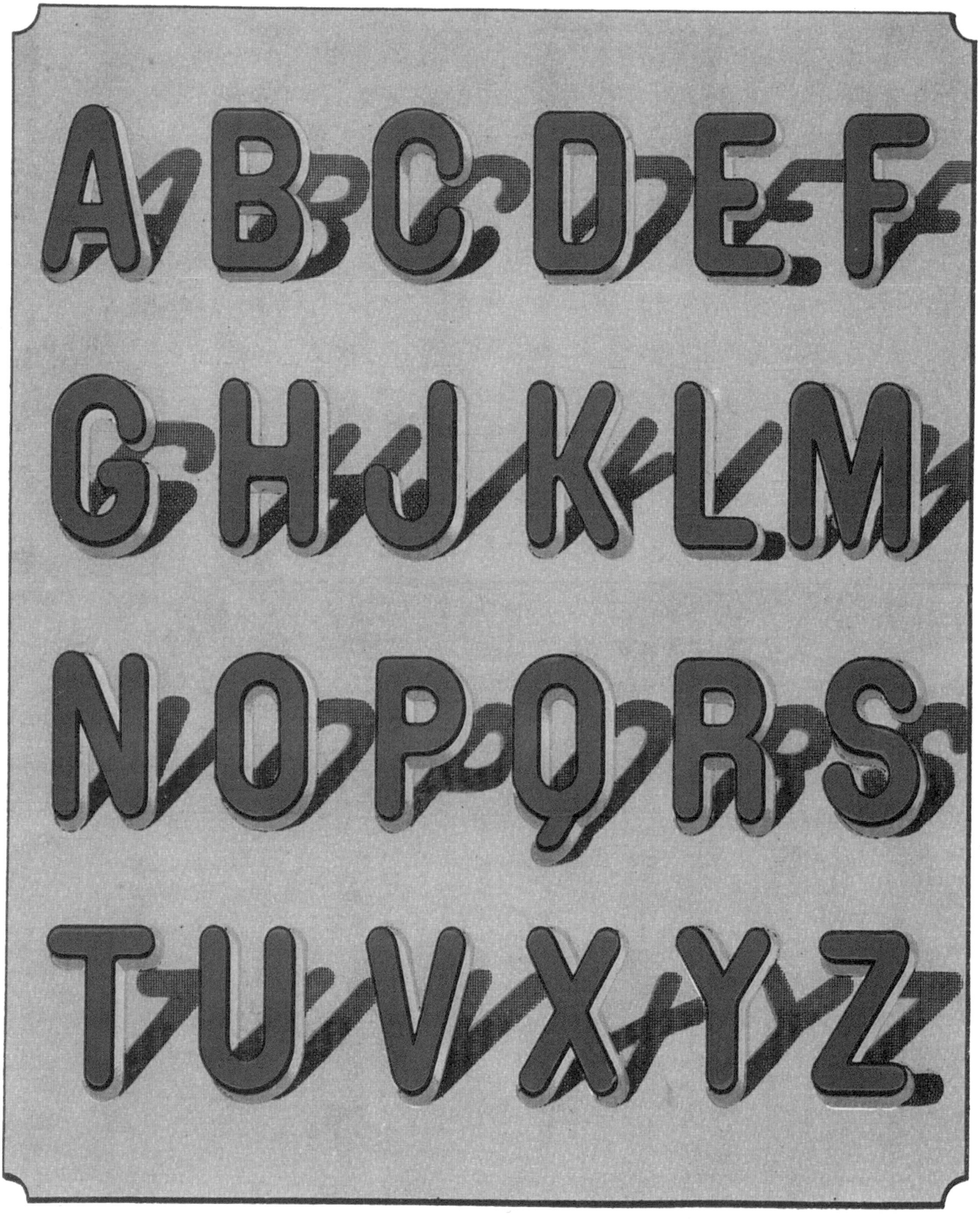
ABCDEF
GHJKLM
NOPQRS
TUVXYZ

TESA

VETROFLEX

NAGO NAGO

HEBERLEIN

+GF+

LABEL

AGENCY GOTHIC

ABCDEFGHI
JKLMNOPQR
STUVWXYZ

1234567890
&.:;-`'!?$¢

le mot.

N° 1. — 1re Année   Deuxième Édition. — 10 Centimes   28 Novembre 1914.

DESSIN DE PAUL IRIBE

David et Goliath

abcdefghijk
lmnopqrſst
uvwxyz

Diese Schablonenschrift ist aus typographischem Material (Messinglinien) entstanden und kann, wie in den hier gezeigten Beispielen 1, 2, 3, systematisch breiter oder höher gemacht werden

a b c. ₁   a b c. ₂

abcdefghik

achtung glas

3

Kunstgewerbeschule Stuttgart (Walter Veit). Schablonenschrift

KONSTRUIERTE SCHRIFTEN

EYE TEST CHARTS

Eye test charts using letters of the alphabet, designed to test visual acuity and the efficacy of corrective lenses, were introduced in the 1830s. To increase optical distance in the testing room, some charts are designed with reversed letters and viewed through a facing mirror. In 1862 the Utrecht optometrist Herman Snellen designed the first scientifically reliable charts for testing vision distance, using carefully size-adjusted letters based on the typeface "Egyptian Paragon". Sans-serif letters, having less visual distraction, were introduced soon after. (Gill Sans Bold has been especially popular with British opticians.) In the 1870s Snellen introduced charts with calibrated lines and abstract figures for young or illiterate patients. Eye test chart designs all over the world are still based on Snellen's pioneering "Optotypes". The economy and clarity demanded by its function gave the eye test chart a typographic formal elegance that was modernist *avant la lettre.*

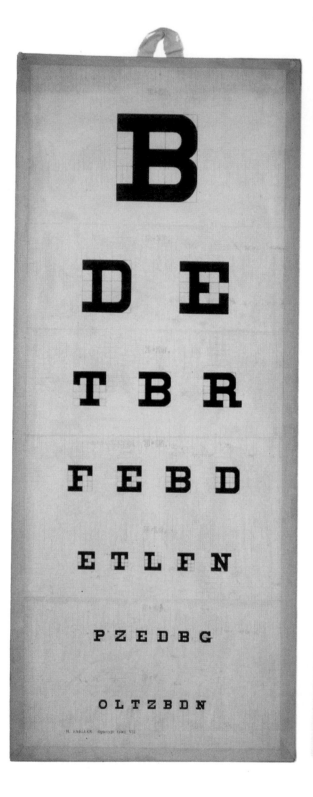

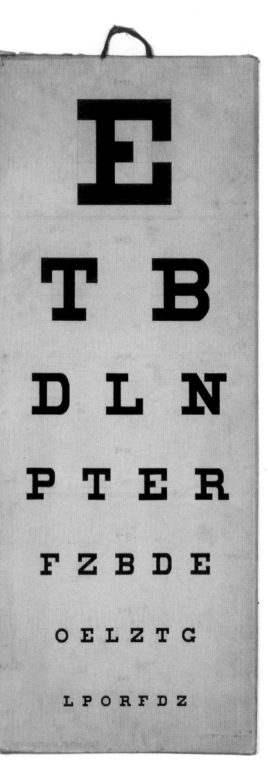

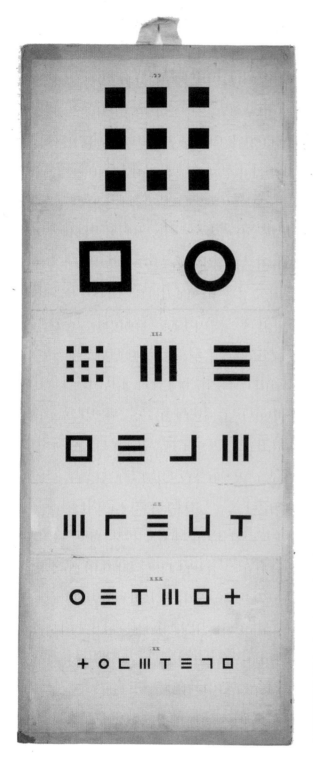
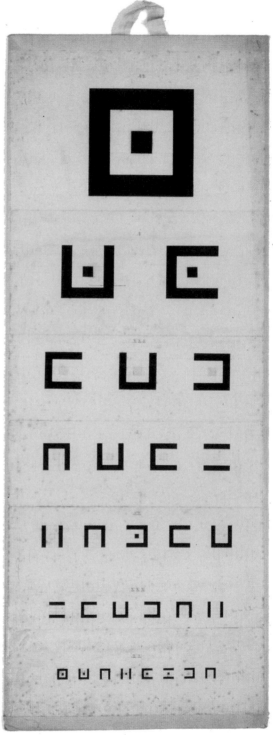

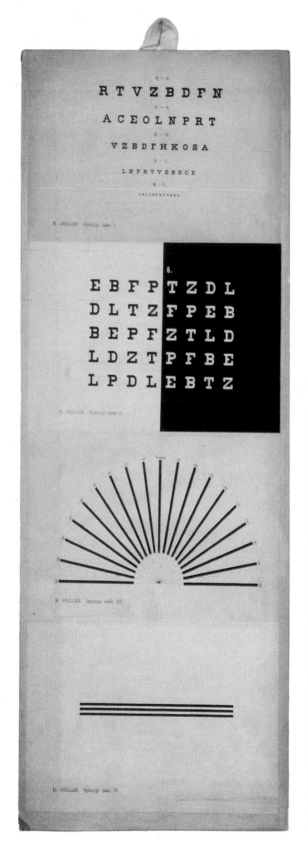

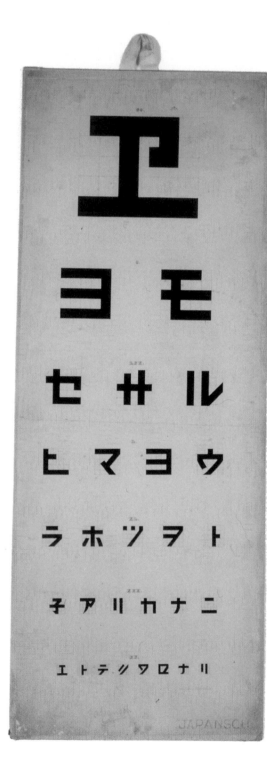
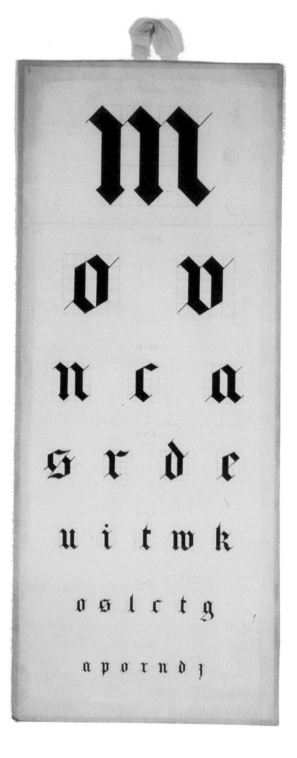

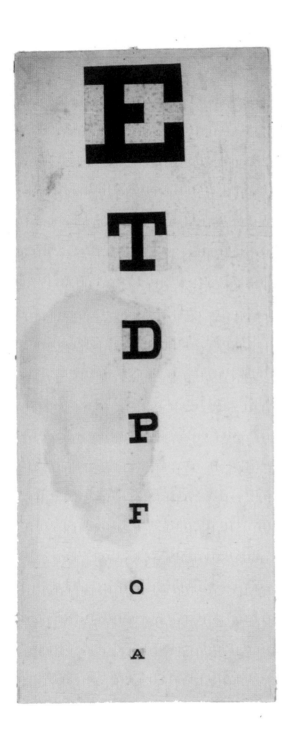
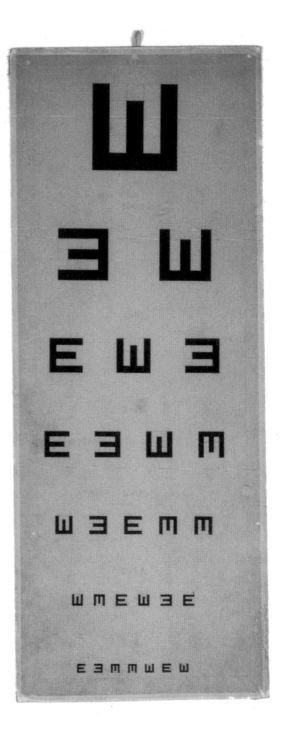

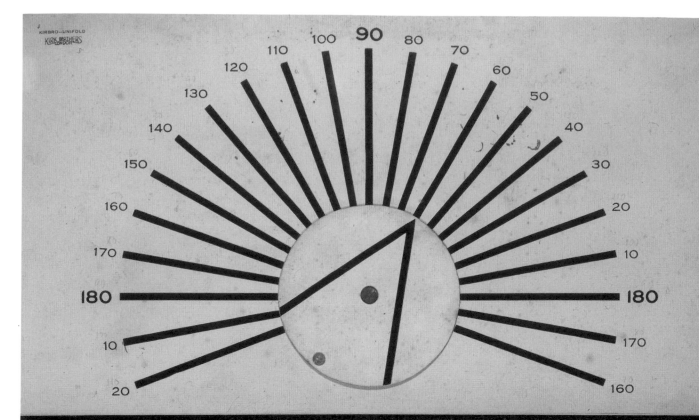

SOCIÉTÉ ANONYME
DES
ÉTABLISSEMENTS
LOUIS
GRASSET
11 RUE TRONCHET ★ PALACIO DE LA MADELEINE
PARIS VIII°. TEL. ANJOU 53-61.53-62.53-63

CONSTRUCTION
GÉNÉRALE
BÉTON
ARMÉ
TRAVAUX
PUBLICS

FONDATIONS

ABCDEFGHIJKLMN
OPQRSTUVWXYZ
ÄÖÜÆŒÇØ$
aabcdefgghijklmɯ
nⅡopqrsſtuvwxyz
æœchckçﬀﬁﬂﬀﬂﬁﬁß
äáàáâäòóôöøùúûü
.,-:;!?('†§*«»&&
1234567890
1234567890
abdegpqréèêëàáâä
åã1238

Corps 48 halbfette Renner Futura * Korrektur 19. Dezember 1927.

Wirtschaftsformen der Erde

Zahnrad: Moderne Wirtschaft (Industrie im Vordergrund)
Hammer: Altkulturwirtschaft (Handwerk und Ackerbau entwickelt)
Pfeil und Bogen: Primitive Wirtschaft (Sammeln, Jagen, primitive Landwirtschaft)

Jede Figur 100 Millionen Menschen Schätzung für 1930

Angefertigt für das Bibliographische Institut AG., Leipzig
Gesellschafts- und Wirtschaftsmuseum in Wien   ©

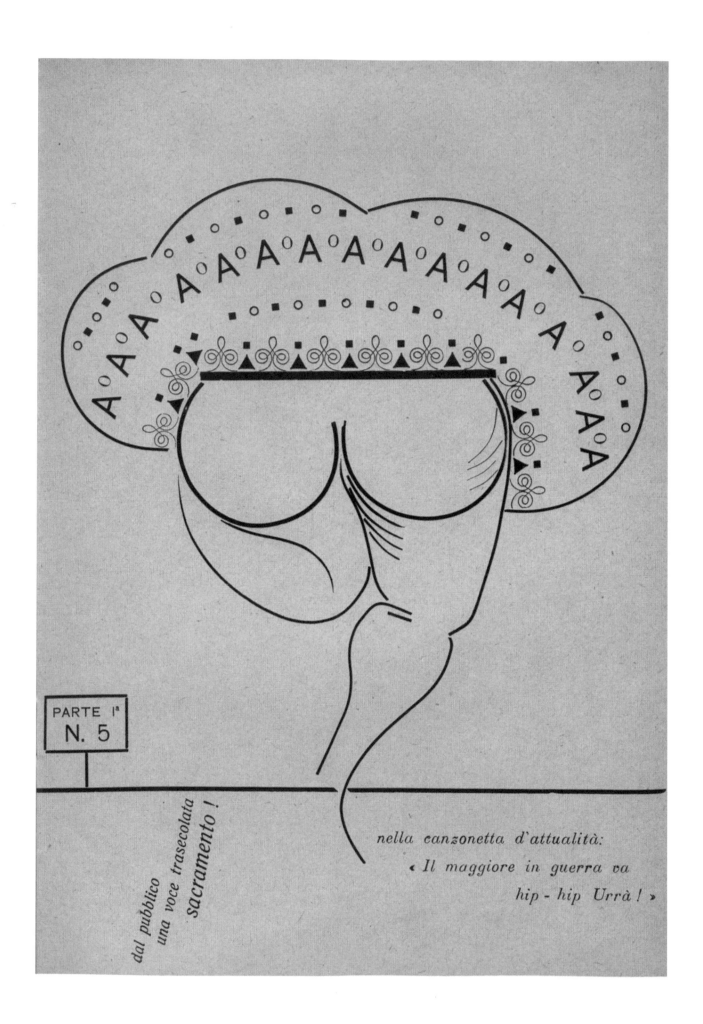

PARTE Iª
N. 5

dal pubblico
una voce trasecolata
sacramento !

nella canzonetta d'attualità:
« Il maggiore in guerra va
hip - hip Urrà ! »

ABCDEFG
HIJKLMN,
OPQRST.
UVWXYZ!
1234567890
abcdefgghij
klmnopqrst
uvwxyÿyz.&?

abcdefghijk
œlmnopqrstu

wxz
ælmnopqrstuy

XYZ

Crous-Vidal, dont l'exposition à la Galerie
d'Orsay fut le " clou " graphique de la ren-
trée 52, a dédié à Jean Giono et à l'école de
Lure ce flamboyant caractère d'inspiration
méditerranénne :
LES CATALANES

LES CATALANES

ISCANRD123

FGHJKLMOPTUV

114

XXe SIECLE Nº 4

XXth CENTURY

EDITION IN ENGLISH

CHRISTMAS 1938

FURNITURE SALE

120 Point 3A

BIG RUG

96 Point 3A

NEW IRON

84 Point 4A

FINE HOUSE

72 Point 5A

LARGE ROOM

Characters in Complete Font

ABCDEFGHIJKL
MNOPQRSTUV
WXYZ&.,.-':.;!?

Fonted and sold separately:

$1234567890

Figures—72 to 144 point

AKMNS

Grotesque Characters—72 to 144 point

FORUM maandblad voor architectuur en gebonden kunsten

12/1953

KESTNER-GESELLSCHAFT
E.V. HANNOVER
KÖNIGSTRASSE 8

WINTER

PROGRAMM

1928-1929

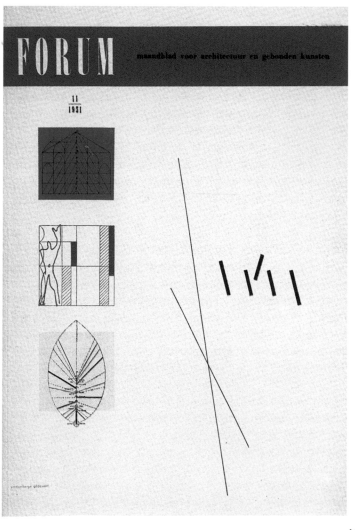

FORUM maandblad voor architectuur en gebonden kunsten

11/1951

DER VORBILDLICHE WERBEDRUCK

ПЯТИЛЕТКА КАДРОВ ОБЩЕСТВЕННОГО ПИТАНИЯ

Заведующих столовыми и их заместителей 6600

Директоров фабрик кухонь и их заместителей 957

Экономистов, работн. т.н.б. и старш. бухгалтеров 1.298

Диэтетиков гигиенистов 686

Инженеров химиков 882 Инженеров технологов 882

Квалифицированных рабочих 39.075 рабочих подручных 53.985

ТЕХНИКОВ-МЕХАНИКОВ 1.285
ТЕХНИКОВ КУЛИНАРОВ 9.810

НАРПИТОВЕЦ ПОВЫШАЙ СВОЮ КВАЛИФИКАЦИЮ

А Б В Г Д Е

Ж З И К Л М

Н О П Р С Т

У Ф Х Ц Ч Щ Щ

Ъ Ы З Ю Я

ABCDEFG
HIJKLMNO
PQRSTU
VWXYZ
.,;:""!?-!?
£1234567
890&C

OKTOBER   1928   OCTOBER

GEBRAUCHSGRAPHIK
INTERNATIONAL ADVERTISING ART

HERAUSGEBER * PROF. H. K. FRENZEL * EDITOR

PHÖNIX ILLUSTRATIONSDRUCK UND VERLAG GMBH., BERLIN SW 61, BELLE-ALLIANCE-PLATZ 7-8

Alleinvertreter für die **THE BOOK SERVICE COMPANY** Sole Representative for the
Vereinigten Staaten von United States of North-
Nordamerika und Kanada 15 East 40th Street, New York City U.S.A. America and Canada

ĀBCDEFGHI
JKLMNŌPQ
RSTŪVWXY
Z I 2 3 4
5 6 7 8 9 0

le témoin.

DIRECTEUR PAUL IRIBE N° 59 21 AVRIL 1935 LE N° UN FRANC

ENFIN, UNE CONFÉRENCE QUI NE FINIT PAS

EN QUEUE DE POISSON...

ABCDEFG
HIJKLŁM
NOPRST
U·W·Y·Z

· 1234567890 ·

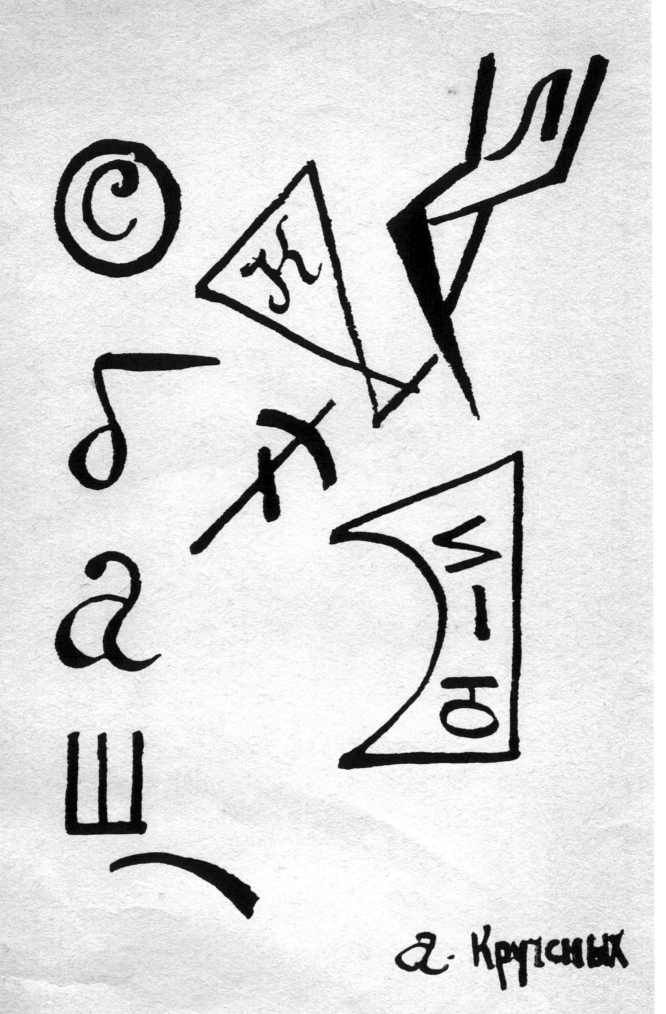

а. Крученых

AAAAAAAABB
CCCDDDEEEFF
GGHHIJJKKK
LLLMMMMNN
NNOOPPPQRRS
STTUUUUUVV
IJWWWXXYYZ&
1234567890
(.,:,"!§?';-)

ИЛЬЯ ЗДАНЕВИЧ
зохна и женихи

130

ČTYŘCICERO „PATRONA" GROTESK RUSKÉ

А Б В Г Д Е Ж З И
А   БВ   ВV   ГО   ДD   Е   ЖŽ   ЗZ   ИI   I

Й К Л М Н О П Р С
ЙJ   К   ЛL   М   НN   О   ПР   РR   СS

Т У Ф Х Ц Ч Ш Щ Ъ
Т   УU   ФF   ХCH   ЦC   ЧČ   ШŠ   ЩŠČ   Ъ

Ы Ь Ѣ Э Ю Я Ѳ Ѵ
ЫY   Ь   Ѣ   ЭE   ЮJU   ЯJA   ѲF   ѴI neb Y

Љ Њ Ћ Ђ Ј Џ Ж Ꙗ
ЉLJ   ЊŇ   ЋТ   ЂĎ   ЈJ   ЏDŽ   ЖA   ЊJA

В. А. ФРАНЦЕВЪ
ПРАГА

131

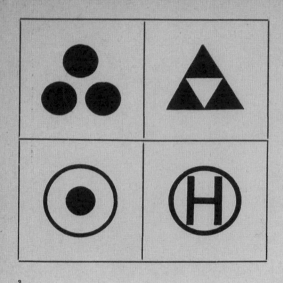

3

4

5

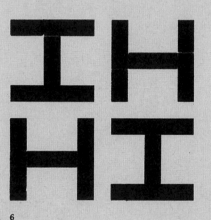

6

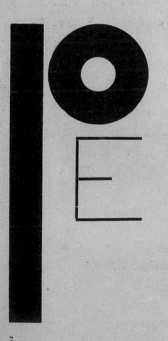

7

3 Japanische Firmenzeichen. Die klaren, geometrischen Grundformen dieser Marken sind vorbildlich für die Gestaltung eines Signets.

4 Die japanische Flagge (Symbol der Sonne)

5 HERBERT BAYER, Typosignet, 2 Varianten. Beim zweiten Zeichen stehen an Stelle der Buchstaben Gedankenstriche.

6 JOHANNES MOLZAHN, Typosignet für eine Eisenwarenfabrik.

7 KURT SCHWITTERS, Typosignet für das Wort Pelikan.

134

NEW LETTER: The signs and symbols of musical notation inspired the design of this new letter-face, which has just been announced. It was designed by Alexey Brodovitch, art director of *Harper's Bazaar* and *Portfolio*, who calls it the Albro Alphabet (after the first syllables of his name). It is being released through Photo-Lettering, Inc., New York.

encres simili-creux

LEFRANC

LEFRANC

ROLAND
ANSIEAU

18

Model S ¾″ Machine cuts this size stencil, one to four lines, any length. For marking medium sized shipments. Size of Machine 21″ x 16″ x 10″ high. Weight 100 lbs. Packed 145 lbs.

Size of Stencil Board for Model S ¾″ Machine

1-line 3″ x 20″	3-line 5″ x 20″
2-line 4″ x 20″	4-line 6″ x 20″

This is an actual reproduction of the stencil characters cut by Model S (¾″ size) Marsh Stencil Machine.

¾″

ABCDEFGHIJ
KLMNOPQRST
UVWXYZ'/&,
234567890-.

This is an actual reproduction of the stencil characters cut by the Model R (1″ size) Marsh Stencil Machine.

Model R 1″ Machine cuts this size, one to four lines, any length. For marking large shipments. Size of machine 24″ x 18″ x 10″ high. Weight 145 lbs. Packed 195 lbs.

Size of Stencil Board for Model R 1″ Machine.

1-line 4″ x 20″ or 24″	3-line 6″ x 20″ or 24″
2-line 5″ x 20″ or 24″	4-line 7″ x 20″ or 24″

1″

ABCDEFGHIJ
KLMNOPQRST
UVWXYZ'/&,
234567890-.

19

15314 - H

15311 - F

15312 - H

15313 - F

1695 - E

10129 — G

7211 — G

10140 — G

8022 — G

8020 — G

8021 — G

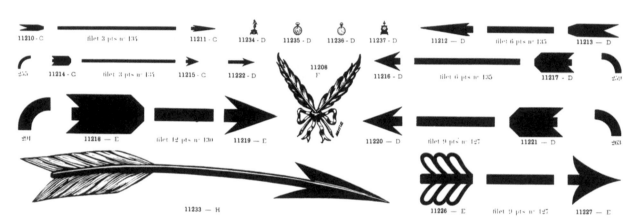

ÉTOILES BLANCHES & NOIRES

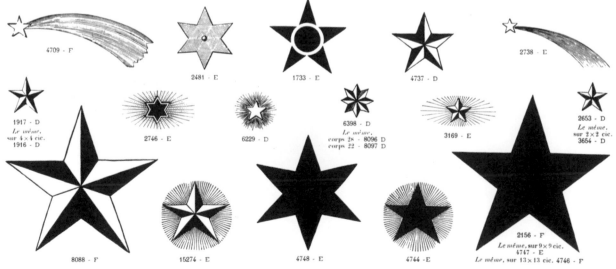

Voir à la 6ᵉ Division du CATALOGUE GÉNÉRAL (page 214), nos ÉTOILES BLANCHES & NOIRES de DIFFÉRENTES DIMENSIONS

A B C D E
F G H I J K
L M N O P
Q R S T U
V W X Y Z

Wij garandeeren
bij afkoeling na verwarming
van den kabel een

V lakke
karakteristiek

20

en **tóch**

een S O E P E L E N kabel

ELECTRICITEIT BOUWT STEDEN

Aenne Biermann

60 **Fotos**   mit Einleitung von Franz Roh   **»Der literarische Foto-Streit«**
60 **photos**   with introduction by Franz Roh **"The literary dispute about photography"**
60 **photographies** avec introduction par Franz Roh **«La querelle au sujet de la photographie»**

Fototek 2   Klinkhardt & Biermann · Verlag · Publishers · Editeurs · Berlin W 10

L. Moholy-Nagy

60 Fotos
60 photos
60 photographies

Fototek 1   Klinkhardt & Biermann · Verlag · Publishers · Editeurs · Berlin W 10

I N M P U V W Z X UM ZU
C E O a S warten am
l f h k d b ß finden; er.
J p q j jammer: gegen
I H A V W N M X Y Hafen
X L F T E Z Formenlehre
J U P B R S O Q C G D !
MOND „INDIEN" CUBA
(1234567890) – & = ?
Geschichte über römisches
Staatsrecht. Zeichenschulen
Grundriss der Anatomie des Menschen
Reise durch Rumänien und Russland.

A

ABRICOT

APRICOT

a

APRIKOSE

G. KARQUEL ★ ALPHABET PHOTOGRAPH

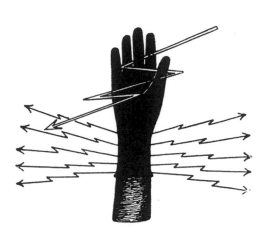

गिनती

१०	९	८	७	६	५	४	३	२	१
२०	१९	१८	१७	१६	१५	१४	१३	१२	११
३०	२९	२८	२७	२६	२५	२४	२३	२२	२१
४०	३९	३८	३७	३६	३५	३४	३३	३२	३१
५०	४९	४८	४७	४६	४५	४४	४३	४२	४१
६०	५९	५८	५७	५६	५५	५४	५३	५२	५१
७०	६९	६८	६७	६६	६५	६४	६३	६२	६१
८०	७९	७८	७७	७६	७५	७४	७३	७२	७१
९०	८९	८८	८७	८६	८५	८४	८३	८२	८१
१००	९९	९८	९७	९६	९५	९४	९३	९२	९१

Published by : INDIAN BOOK DEPOT, DELHI-110 006.
Printed at INDIAN ART PRESS, NEW DELHI-110 064.

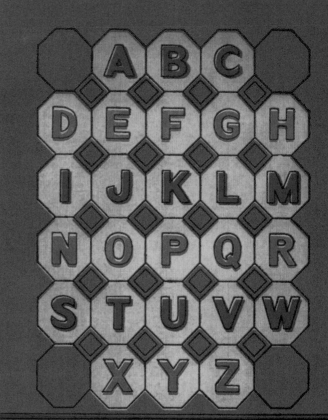

A B C
D E F G H
I J K L M
N O P Q R
S T U V W
X Y Z

Publishers:
INDIAN BOOK DEPOT
2937, Bahadur Garh Rd.
Delhi-110006

Printers:
INDIAN ART PRESS
A/6, Mayapuri,
New Delhi-110064.

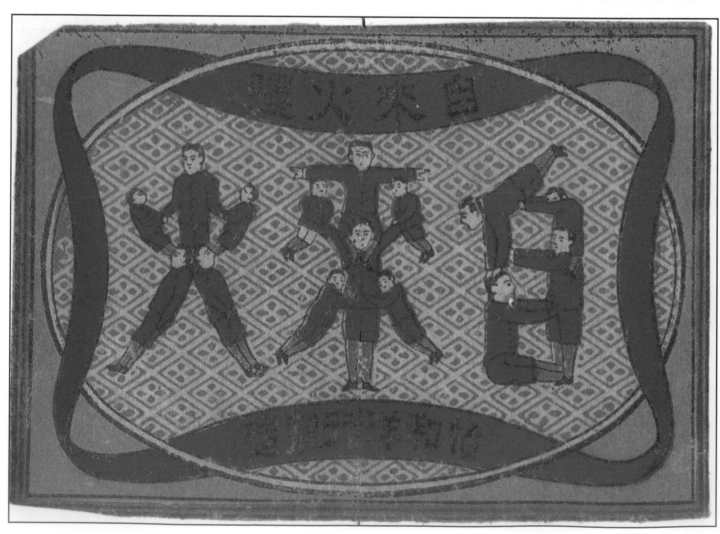

144

ab

bbcddef
ghChrijkklmn
noppqqrrss
tuvwwxgyyz

3039

3040

3041

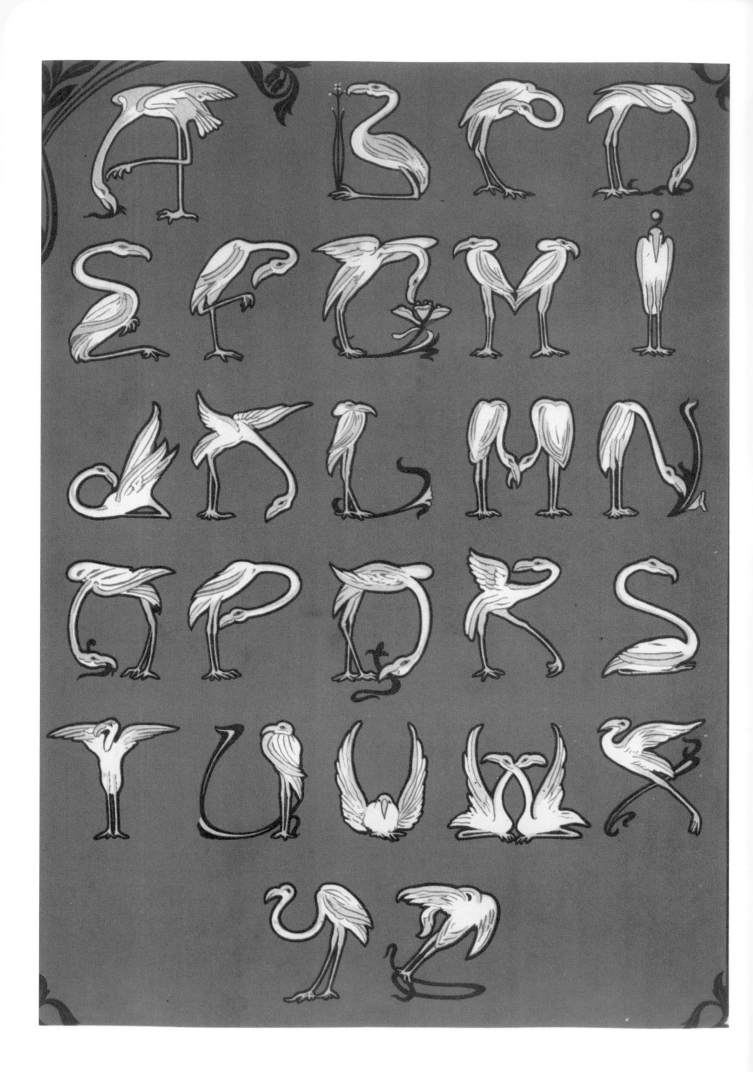

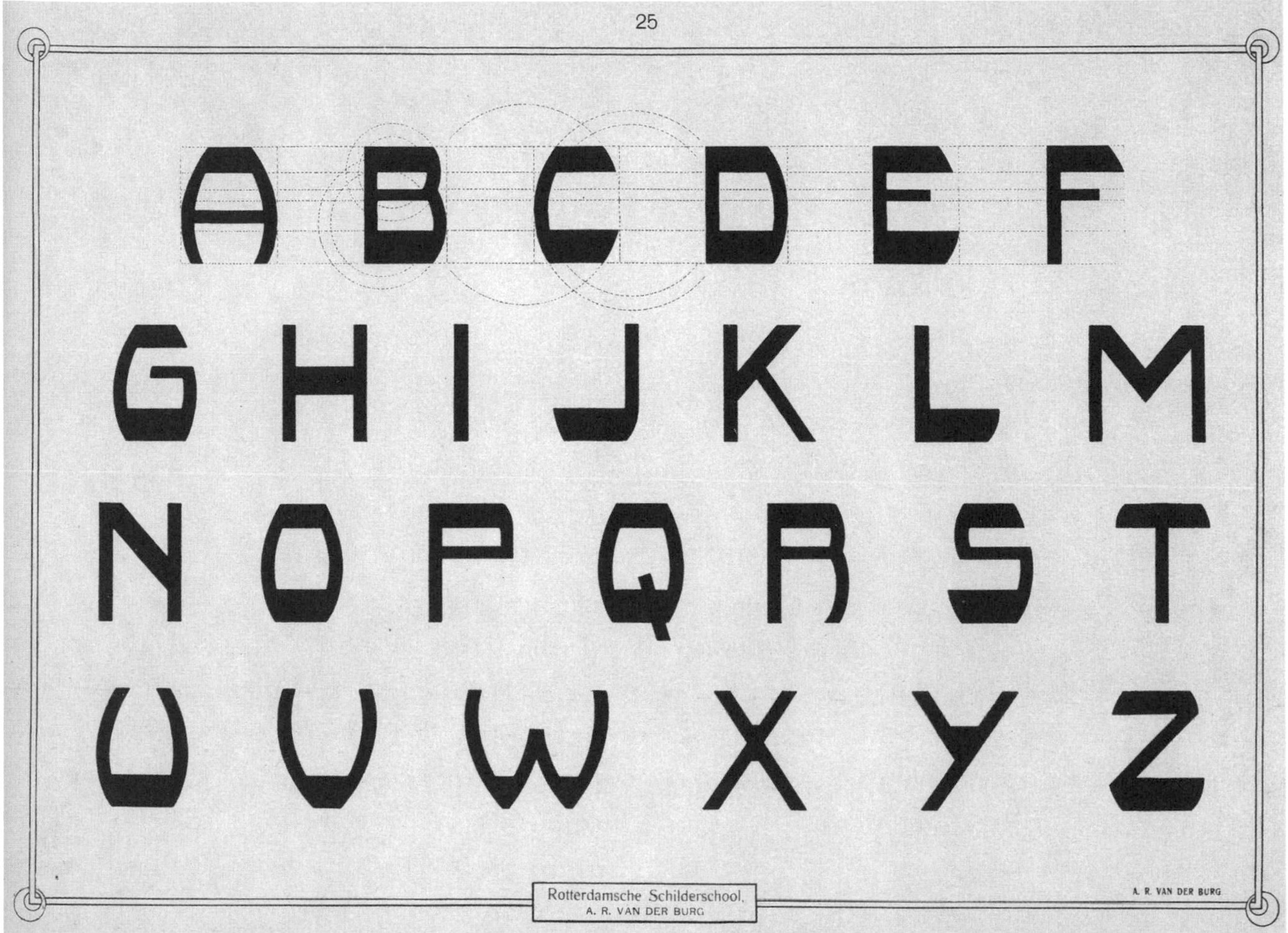

ABCDEF
GHIJKLM
NOPQRST
UVWXYZ

Rotterdamsche Schilderschool.
A. R. VAN DER BURG

A. R. VAN DER BURG

ABCDEF
GHIJKLM
NOPQRST
UVWXYZ

Rotterdamsche Schilderschool.
A. R. VAN DER BURG.

A. R. VAN DER BURG.

abcdefghij
klmnopqr
stuvwxyz
1234567890

Rotterdamsche Schilderschool,
A. R. VAN DER BURG.

A. R. VAN DER BURG.

abcdefghi
jklmnopqr
stuvwxyz
1234567890

Rotterdamsche Schilderschool,
A. R. VAN DER BURG

A. R. VAN DER BURG.

ATLAS

AZTLAN

IMP, Y LIT, ESPAÑOLA

MÉXICO.

MDCCCLXXXV.

COZCATECUTLAN.	COZOHUÍPILECAN.	CUACHQUETZALOYAN.

CUAHUACAN.	CUAHUITLIXCO.	CUAHXOMULCO.

CUALAC.	CUATLATAUCH.	CUATZONTEPEC.
		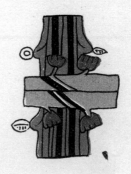
CUAUHNACAZTLAN.	CUAUHNAHUAC.	CUAUHPANOAYAN.

151

ABCDEFGHIJK
LMNOPQRSTU
VWXYZ0&&&
abcdefghijklmno
pqrstuvwxyz000
1234567890O$

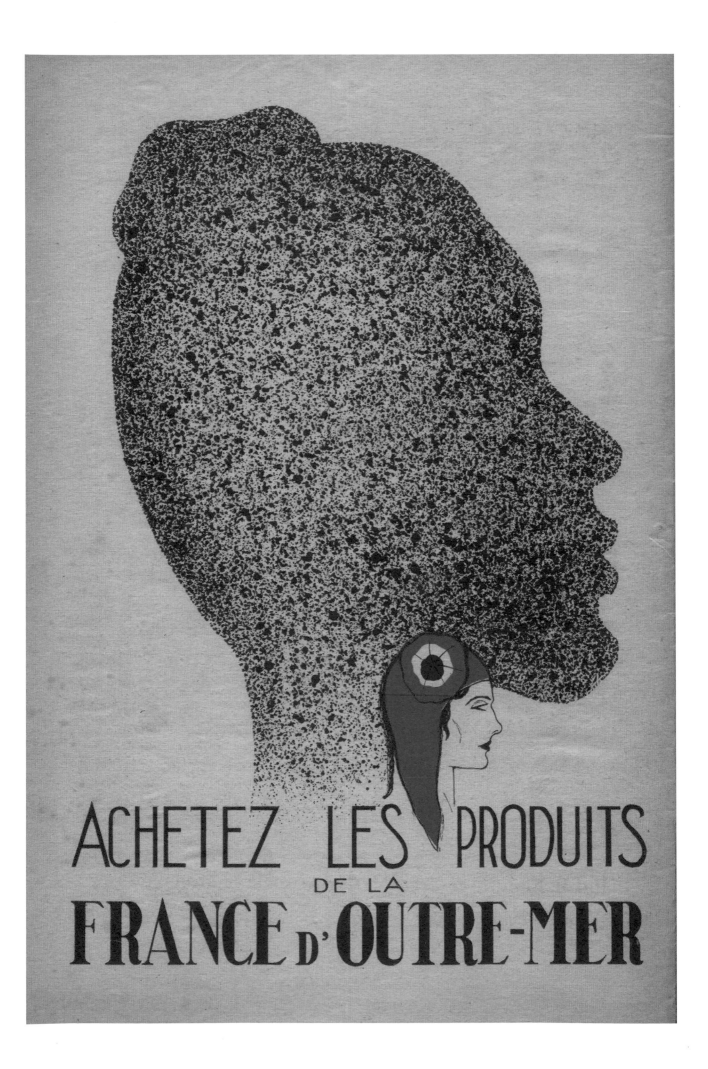

ACHETEZ LES PRODUITS
DE LA
FRANCE D'OUTRE-MER

EXPOSITION D'ART MEXICAIN
ANCIEN ET MODERNE

MUSEE NATIONAL D'ART MODERNE
PARIS · MAI-JUILLET 1952

MEXICO en el ARTE
número 12

OPeRa
NACIONAL
con la COLABORACION del INBA
1951

ARAGÓN

A B C D E F G H I

J K L M N Ñ O P Q

R S T U V W X Y Z

Æ . , ; : Œ

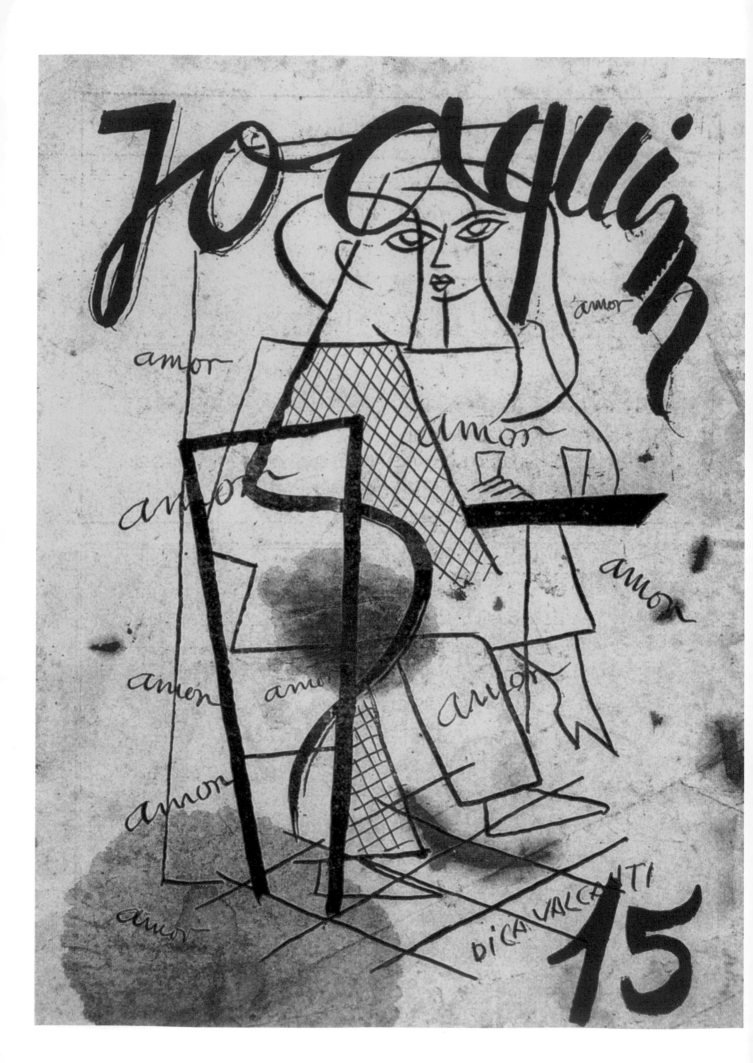

ABCDEFF

GGHMIJK

LMNOPQ

PPRSTU

VWXYY

SC

AX

PQ

FL

FF

MODÈLES DE

GP

JEAN PUIFORCAT

NA

GD

ARTS ET METIERS GRAPHIQUES

LETTRES

18 RUE SEGUIER PARIS 6

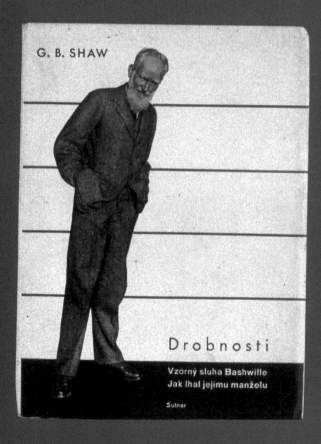

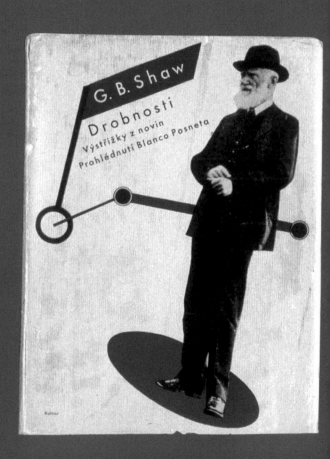

A CZECH MODERNIST ALPHABET

Karel Teige (1900-1951) was the greatest of the Czech avant-garde artist-writers of the 1920s and 1930s. His 1926 photomontage designs for the twenty-four-poem sequence *Abeceda*, written by his friend Vítezslav Nezval, are a uniquely elegant and witty invention, one of the enduring achievements of Czech modernism. The designs feature the third collaborator in the project, the dancer Milca Mayarová, whose idea it was to choreograph the poems, creating a pose for each letter, and then to publish the book with Teige's title designs. Using Karel Paspa's photographs of Mayarová, which contrive to be both erotic and chastely gymnastic, Teige's designs transform the alphabet into what is effectively a constructivist manifesto, a demonstration of his aim to create a new "optical language, a system of signs capable of embodying words in graphic figures." It is a stunning realisation of what László Moholy-Nagy had called for in his influential 1925 Bauhaus book, *Painting, Photography, Film*, the dynamic combination of photographic image and lettering he termed "typofoto." Like Mayarová, Teige succeeds in finding an utterly original and distinctive solution for every letter: her brilliant pose alphabet is animated into a visual dance, what Nezval called "a living poem."

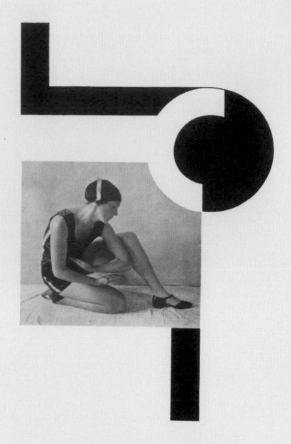

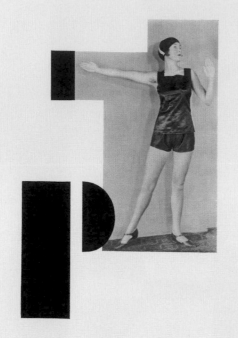

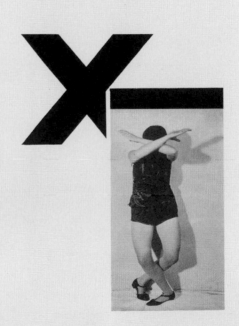

Cancer ♋

Decan III

ABCDEFGHI
JKLMNOPQR
STUVWXYZ
1234567890
·REVOLUTION·
·WASHINGTON·

ABCDEFGHIJ
KLMNOPQRS
TUVWXYZ
1234567890
aabcdefghijklm
nopqrstuvwxyz

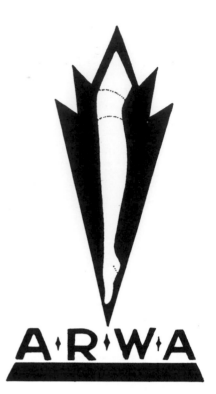

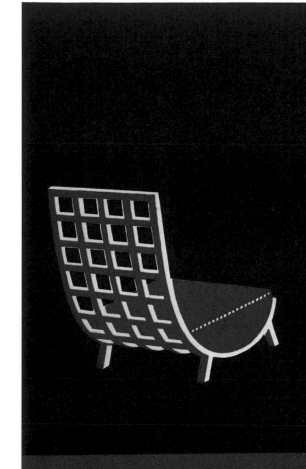

KOZMA.

EINZELMÖBEL
UND NEUZEITLICHE
RAUMKUNST

HERAUSGEGEBEN
VON ALEXANDER
KOCH DARMSTADT

ЕЖИПТИЕН

А Б В Г

Д Е Ж З И

К Л М Н О

П Р С Т У Ф Х

Ц Ч Ш Щ

Ъ Ь Ю Я

---

1 2 3 4 5 6 7

8 9 & 9 0

| werbe-
entwurf
und ausführung | dessau, bauhaus
d | herbert-bayer
b |

das wesentliche einer aufgabe muß erforscht und erkannt werden, dann wird die äußere erscheinung einer werbsache das logische mittel sein zum zweck, den die werbsache erfüllen soll. eine arbeit nach dieser auffassung verbürgt überzeugungskraft und qualität. alle darstellungsmittel der typografie, fotografie, malerei, zeichnung . . . . . wende ich zweckmäßig an bei: warenzeichen, geschäftspapier, inserat, prospekt, plakat, packung, werbebau und anderen werbsachen. weite technischen kenntnisse und erfahrungen sichern eine wirtschaft-

vdr-kartei der
werbindustrie
februar 1928

abcdefghi
jklmnopqr
stuvwxyz

d

HERBERT BAYER: Abb. 1. Alfabet
„g" und „k" sind noch als
unfertig zu betrachten

**Beispiel eines Zeichens
in größerem Maßstab
Präzise optische Wirkung**

sturm blond

Abb. 2. Anwendung

399

A B C D E F G H I J K L M N O P Q R
S T U V W X Y Z ★ 1 2 3 4 5 6 7 8 9 ★ ?

a b c d e f g h i j k l m
n o p q r s t u v w x y z

VARIETY
·
VARIETY

− it's the RESULT that COUNTS !

A B C D E F G H I J K L
M N O P Q R S T U V W X
Y Z 1 2 3 4 5 6 7 8 9 ?

VARIETY

A B C D E F G H I J K L
M N O P Q R S T U V W
X Y Z 1 2 3 4 5 6 7 8 9

VARIETY

LABELS THAT SAY "TRY ME"

Business goes to him that asks for it.

The inefficient label says "I'm Jones' Tea."

The sales producing label proudly proclaims "I'm Jones' tasty, savory tea," and shows by its appropriate dress that it is a product from the distant, romantic Orient, land of spices and temples.

Labels designed by Wurzburg Brothers are busy all the time—making good impressions—creating sales—and insisting that Mr. and Mrs. Consumer "Try Me."

Send your label, carton and wrapper problems to our Printed Products Division for skillful and experienced aid in producing "Sales Assisting" designs.

GOLDEN TEMPLE

ORANGE PEKOE

TEA

WURZBURG BROTHERS, Memphis, Tenn.

DESIGNERS AND SUPPLIERS: PAPER LABELS—FOIL LABELS—CARTONS—PRINTED WRAPS.

F. C. WEISKOPF

DO XXI. STOLETÍ
PŘESTOUPIT!

ODEON

O 74

日刊ゲンダイ

89. 5. 18

71

18線

渋谷

峰村東即殿

S20125

2個口

月木B版

50部

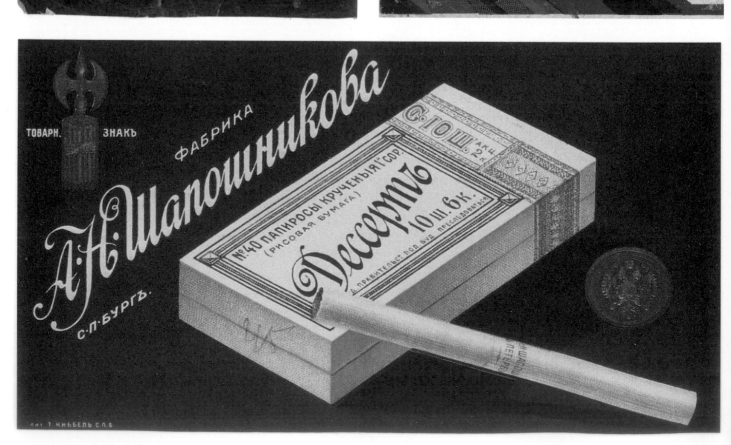

ДРЕВНЕ—СЛАВАНСКИЙ АЛФАВИТ
XVII ←•→ XIX

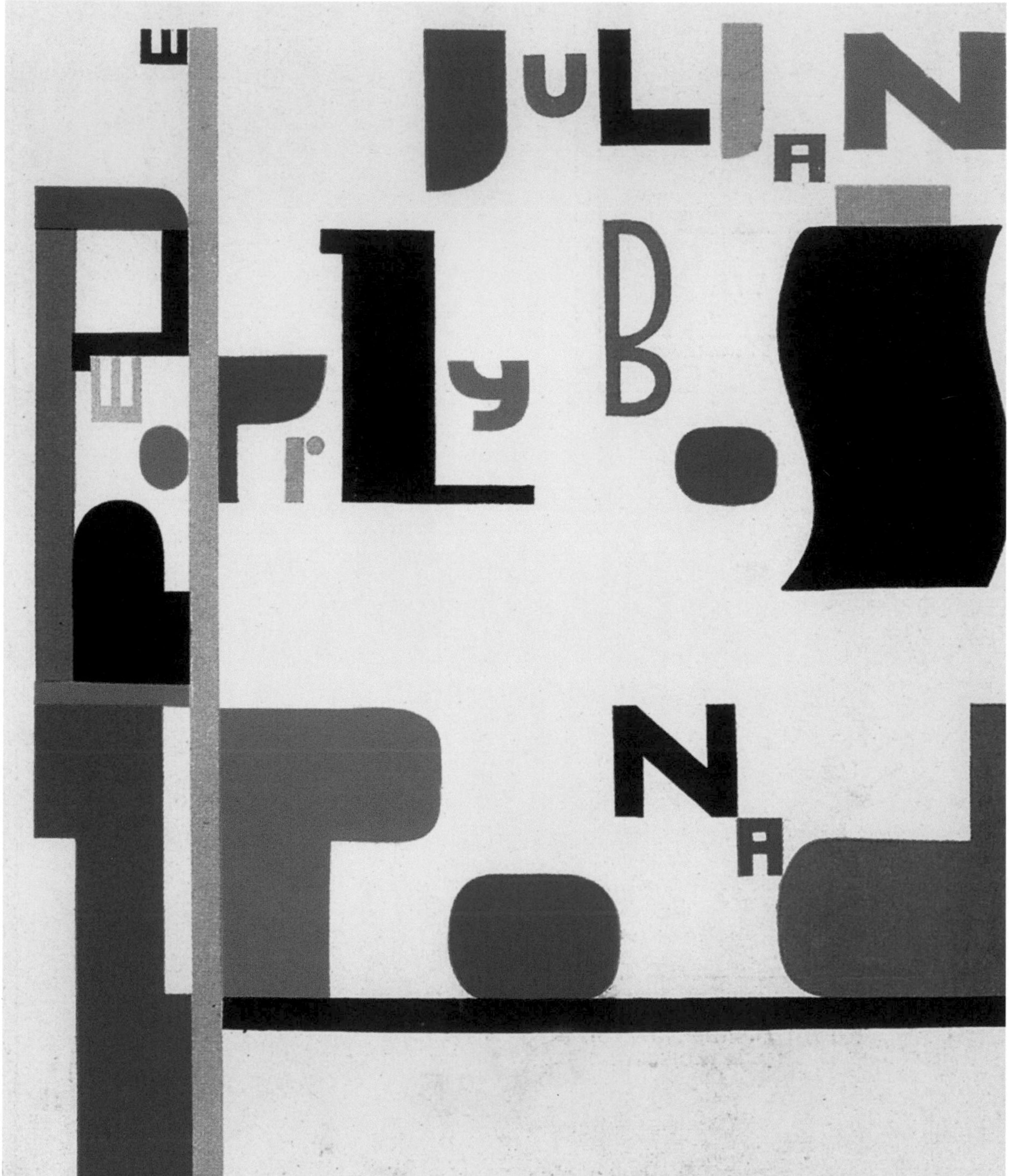

aaaaabbbbc
ddefgghiij
klmnnoooppp
qqırrſstuv
wxxyz

TIPPLER

Dusk to Dawn in the life of a Man-about-town, as shown by twenty-six different scenes, each decorating a letter of this tippler alphabet.

RENÉ AHRLÉ

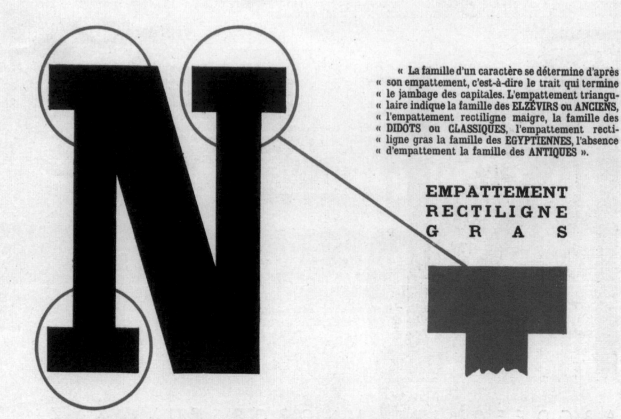

EMPATTEMENT
RECTILIGNE
G R A S

ABCDEFGHIJKLM
NOPQRSTUVWXYZ

abcdefghijklm
nopqrstuvwxyz

1234567890

TYPE D'EGYPTIENNE : LA COMPACTE

L'ART DE RECONNAITRE UN CARACTÈRE
(PRINCIPE DE THIBAUDEAU)

FAÇADE

la façade, hermétiquement fermée, de cet immeuble de bureaux, chauffé et ventilé par l'air conditionné, sera employée à des fins publicitaires.

en avant de cette façade fermée, mais vitrée, à un mètre ou 1m.50 environ, sera fixé une sorte de canevas métallique, sur lequel on pourra accrocher n'importe quel placard publicitaire : (lettres, chiffres, affiches, écran de cinéma, etc.)

le canevas métallique sera équipé d'un réseau électrique destiné aux réclames lumineuses.

une telle façade publicitaire pourrait se louer en entier ou par fraction, par jour, semaine ou mois, suivant l'organisation prévue par le loueur de cette façade.

au-dessus de la façade publicitaire, se trouve l'atelier de préparation des différents placards à accrocher sur la façade, ateliers comportant des espaces aménagés pour les différents spécialistes (peinture, tôlerie, serrurerie, menuiserie, électricité, etc...)

ces placards sont amenés jusque devant l'alignement du canevas métallique par des rails suspendus et sont descendus à hauteur voulue.

entre la façade et le panneau métallique, à chaque étage, par exemple, des passerelles permettent aux ouvriers le montage et le démontage des placards tandis que des échelles assurent les communications verticales.

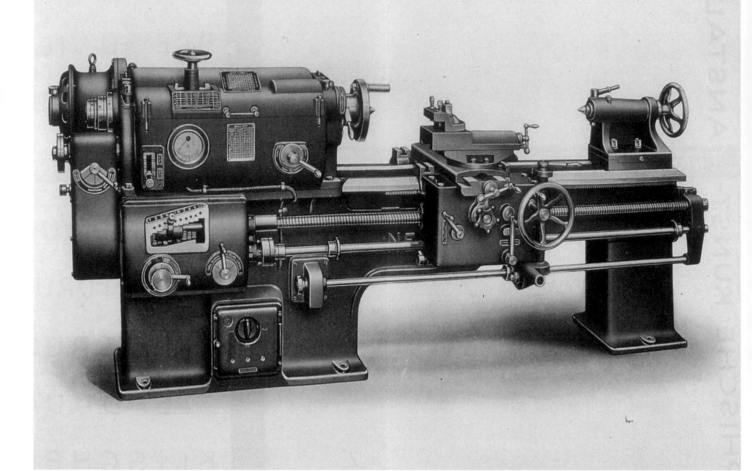

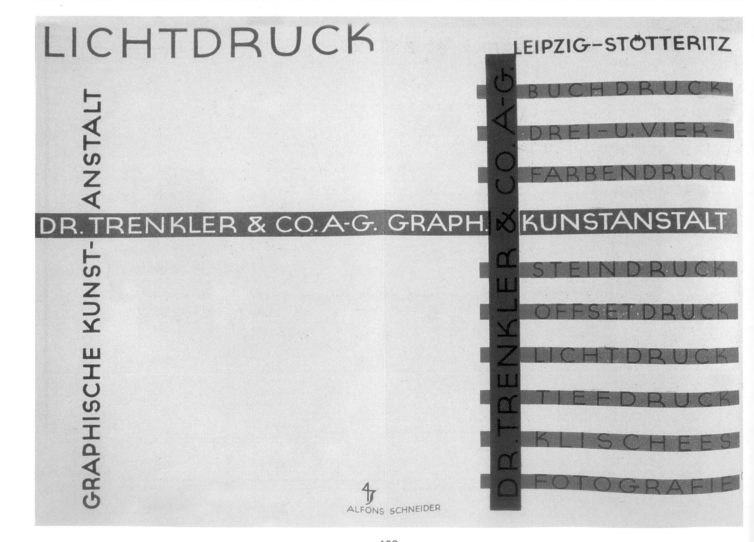

LICHTDRUCK

GRAPHISCHE KUNST- ANSTALT

DR. TRENKLER & CO. A-G. GRAPH. KUNSTANSTALT

LEIPZIG—STÖTTERITZ

BUCHDRUCK

DREI-U.VIER-

FARBENDRUCK

STEINDRUCK

OFFSETDRUCK

LICHTDRUCK

TIEFDRUCK

KLISCHEES

FOTOGRAFIE

DR. TRENKLER & CO. A-G.

ALFONS SCHNEIDER

198

VWMNK
OCSQGA
XYZIEFL
UDBRP
JTH;,!?:

ABCDEFGHIJ
KLMNOPQRS
TUVWXYZ$!?
1234567890

AA B CC DD
EE FF G HH
I J K LL M
NN O PP Q
RR SS TT UU
V W X Y Z
Æ Œ Ç & Cᵉ

( ) . , : ; ' - « » ! ?

1 2 3 4 5 6 7 8 9 0

le mot.

N° 17. — 1ʳᵉ Année.   30 Centimes.   Samedi 1ᵉʳ Mai 1915.

DESSIN DE PAUL IRIBE.

LA VEILLÉE DES NEUTRES.

FUTURA
die Schrift unserer Zeit
BEGLEITE
das Bild unserer Zeit

MILANO

206

ABCDEFGHIJ
JKLMNOPQR
STUVWXYZ
abcdefghi
jklmnopqrsß
tuvwxyz
MOTORRÄDER

abcdefghijk

lmnopqrſstu

vnxyz

aaaaaaß

This type is set with typographical material (Brass Rule). The letter ‹a› below shows how the individual pieces are assembled.

graphische abteilung der

nürttembergischen

staatlichen

A specimen showing the possibilities in letter formation

kunstgenuerbeschule stuttgart

School of decorative Art, Stuttgart. Brass Rule Letters

CONSTRUCTED LETTERS

A B C D E F
G H i J K L M
N O P Q R S
T U U V W X
Y Z

DIE
Cenci

DEUTSCHE
OPAK
GLAS
WERKE

abcdefghijklmno
pqrsstuvwxyz

ABCDEFGHIJKLMN
OPQRSTUVWXYZ

KONSTRUIERTE SCHRIFTEN

PABLO PICASSO

Voyez ce peintre il prend les choses avec leur ombre aussi et d'un coup d'œil sublimatoire

Il se déchire en accords profonds   et agréables à respirer tel l'orgue que j'aime entendre
Des Arlequines jouent dans le   rose et bleus d'un beau-ciel   Ce souvenir revit
les rêves   et les actives mains   Orient plein de glaciers   L'hiver est rigoureux
Lustres   or toile irisée or   loi des stries de feu   fond en murmurant.
Bleu   flamme légère   argent des ondes   bleues après le grand cri
Tout   en restant   elles touchent   cette sirène violon
Faons   lourdes ailes   l'incandesce   quelques brasses encore
Bourdons   femmes striées   éclat de   plongeon-diamant
Arlequins   semblables à Dieu   en variété   Aussi distingués qu'un lac
Fleurs   brillant comme deux   perles   monstres qui palpitent
Lys   cerclés d'or,   je n'étais pas seul!   fais onduler les remords
     Nouveau monde très matinal   montant de l'énorme mer
     L'aventure de ce vieux cheval   en Amérique
     Au soir de la pêche merveilleuse   l'œil du masque
     Air de petits violons au fond des   anges rangés
Dans le couchant puis au bout de   l'an des dieux
Regarde la tête géante et immense   la main verte
L'argent sera vite remplacé par   tout notre or
Morte pendue à l'hameçon... c'est   la danse bleue
L'humide voix des acrobates   des maisons
Grimace parmi les assauts du vent   qui s'assoupit
Ouis les vagues et le fracas d'une   femme bleue
Enfin la grotte à l'atmosphère dorée   par la vertu
Ce saphir veiné   il faut rire!
Rois de phosphore   sous les arbres les bottines entre des plumes bleues
La danse des   dix mouches   lui fait face quand il songe à toi
Le cadre bleu   tandis que   l'air agile s'ouvrait aussi
     Au milieu des   regrets dans une vaste grotte.
     Prends les araignées roses
     Regrets d'invisibles pièges   à la nage
Paisible se souleva mais sur le clavier   l'air
Guitare-tempête   musiques
O gai trémolo   ô gai trémolo
Il ne rit pas   ô gai trémolo
Ton pauvre   l'artiste-peintre
L'ombre agile   étincellement pâle
Immense désir   d'un soir d'été qui meurt
Je vis nos yeux   et l'aube émerge des eaux si lumineuses
J'entendis sa voix   diamants enfermer le reflet du ciel vert et
L'acrobate à cheval le poète à moustaches un oiseau mort et tant d'enfants sans larmes
     qui dorait les forêts tandis que vous pleuriez
Choses cassées des livres déchirés des couches de poussière et des aurores déferlant!

GUILLAUME APOLLINAIRE

ABCDEFGHIJKLMNOPQRSTUVWXYZ

IMAGES DU MONDE

**MER
MARINES MARINS**

RACES

PAR
PAUL VALÉRY
de l'Académie Française

PAR
JEAN BRUNHES
de l'Institut

Volumes in-quarto écu de 112 pages, illustrés de 96 planches en héliogravure et brochés dans une couverture illustrée en papier fort. Prix : 30 francs. (On souscrit aux 6 premiers volumes de la collection pour 165 francs, payables : 27 fr. 50 à la réception de chaque volume.)

AAABCDEEFFGGHKI
IJKELEMMMMNNNOP
ORRSSTUVUUVWXYZ
1234567890aabccd
effghkmnopqrsßttwyz
GROSSER AUSVERKAUF
Möbelschau Juni 1931

ABCDEFGKLMNPORSTUVUWXZ
Textil·Seide.Wolle.Velvet·3
Porzellan Steingut.Ton.Glas Kristall

Text mit schmal-hohen Großbuchst. ist immer schlecht leserlich, man benutze daher diese Schrift nur mit gr.u-kl-Buchst.

212

AUS DER BUCHGEWERBEABTEILUNG DER HANDWERKER UND KUNSTGEWERBESCHULE BRESLAU

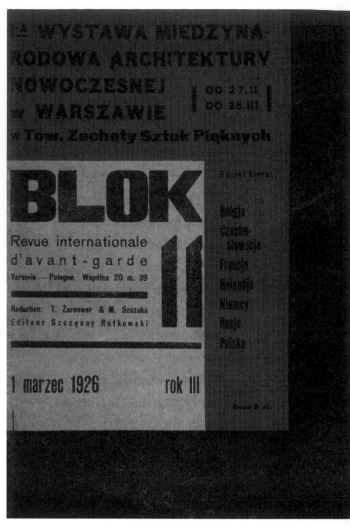

HNBDICRMKE
GOPÁVSYŮWL
JŠTZXFMYJQ

1234567890 2

abrphxfcvdn.
stgmjúyeikz

RETOUR A LA

NAÏVETÉ

EDITIONS

créées et réalisés par

PAUL MARTIAL

SOYEZ FIER DE VOS BEAUX IMPRIMÈS

Pourquoi cache-t-il le dépliant dans une enveloppe de faire-part ?
Pourquoi cache-t-il son nom à la fin d'un texte rédactionnel ?
Pourquoi être astucieux ? Pourquoi être machiavélique ?
Vous êtes fier de ce que vous fabriquez ! Vous êtes fier de ce que vous vendez !
Annoncez-le dès l'enveloppe.

francis
bernard

le mot.

Nº 15 — 1ʳᵉ Année   10 Centimes   Samedi 27 Mars 1915

DESSIN DE PAUL IRIBE.

POURQUOI PAS ?

МЕЛОДИИ
НАРОДОВ

MÉLODIES
DES PEUPLES

для голоса с фортепиано

pour 1 voix et Piano

ВЫПУСК I SÉRIE

АБВГД
ЕЖЗИКЛМ
НОПРСТ
УФХЦЧШ
ЩЪЫЬЮЯ

ABCDEF
GHIJKL!
MNOPQR
STUVW$
XYZ1234
567890&

REVISTA MENSUAL HECHA POR PINTORES, GRABADORES, ESCRITORES, DIBUJANTES, FOTOGRAFOS

1946

JUNIO ● EN DEFENSA DEL PROGRESO SOCIAL DE MEXICO ● PRECIO 50 CVS.

CONSTITUCION POLITICA

GOBIERNO Y FASCISTAS DESGARRAN IMPUNEMENTE LA CONSTITUCION

144 Point
Ludlow 6-EC Gothic Extra Condensed

A B C D E F
G H I J K L M
N O P Q R S T
U V W X

> ### NOTE
> For the remainder of this alphabet, points, figures, other characters, information, etc., see the following page

Y Z & 1 2 3 4

5 6 7 8 9 0 $

£ . : , ; - ' ? !

Nr. 2

WERBEWESEN:

DAS SCHAUFENSTER

„Sie können ruhig Ihren Mittagsschlaf sich gönnen!"

Organisieren Sie Ihre Werbetätigkeit! Die arbeitet für Sie und trägt Gewinn herein, auch wenn Sie schlafen.

Flugblätter mit dem Buntquadrat werden herausgegeben von Max Burchartz. Sie erscheinen bei der Westdeutschen Treuhandgesellschaft Canis & Co., K.-G., Bochum. Sie bringen Aufsätze (meist mit Abbildungen) von Künstlern und Fachleuten über allgemeine und besondere Fragen der Kultur und Organisation, der Baugestaltung, der Formgestaltung von Industrieerzeugnissen und über Werbewesen.

Bewahren Sie jedes „Flugblatt mit einem Buntquadrat" gut auf! Sehen Sie ab u. zu hinein! Es bringt Ihnen Gewinn, sofern Sie seine Ratschläge befolgen.

ABCDE
FGHIJ
KLMNO
PQRST
UVWX
·YZ&·

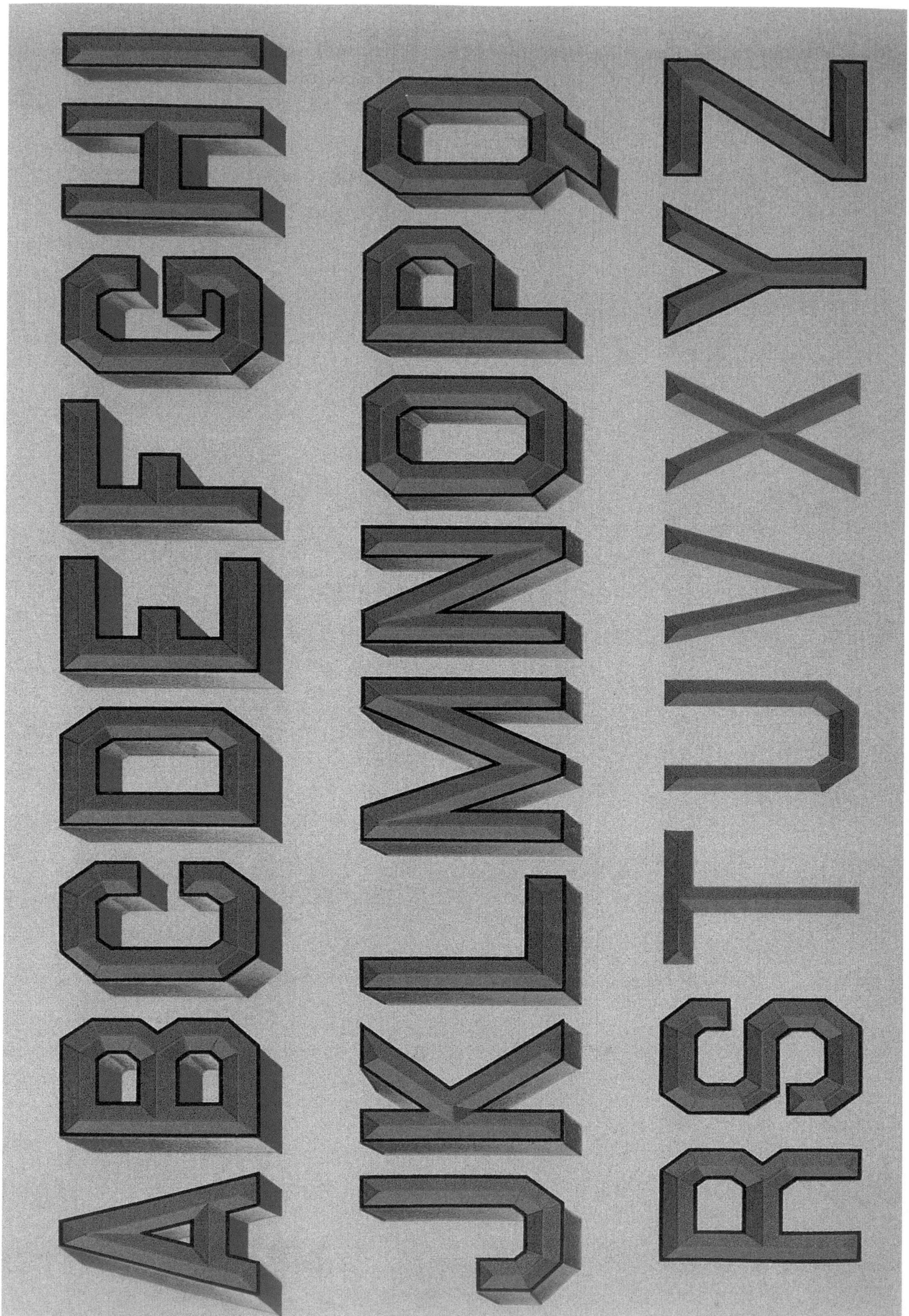
ABCDEFGHI
JKLMNOPQ
RSTUVXYZ

A B C D E F G H I J K
L M N O P Q R S T U V
1 2 3 4 5 6 7 8 9 0
W X Y Z
a b c d e f g h i k l m n o
p q r s t u v w x y z

Fette Kursiv.

ABCDEFGHIJKLMN
OPQRSTUVWXYZ
abcdefghijklmnopqrst
12345 uvwxyz 67890

Kursiv.

BCDEFGHIJKLMNOPQ
RSTUVWXYZ
bcdefghijklmnopqrstuvwxyz
1234567890

Magere enge Antiqua.

ABCDEFGHIJK
LMNOPQRSTU
VWXYZ
abcdefghiklmnopqr
stuvwxyz
1234567890

Fette Antiqua.

ABCDEFGHIJ
KLMNOPQRST
UVWXYZ
abcdefghijk
lmnopqrstuv
wxyz

Enge Antiqua.

BCDEFGHIJ
LMNOPQRST
UVWXYZ
bcdefghijklm
opqrstuvwxyz
1234567890

Breite Antiqua.

ABCDEFGHIJKLMNOPQRSTUV
WXYZ 1234567890
abcdefghijklmnopqrstuvwxyz
Hamburg BRESLAU München

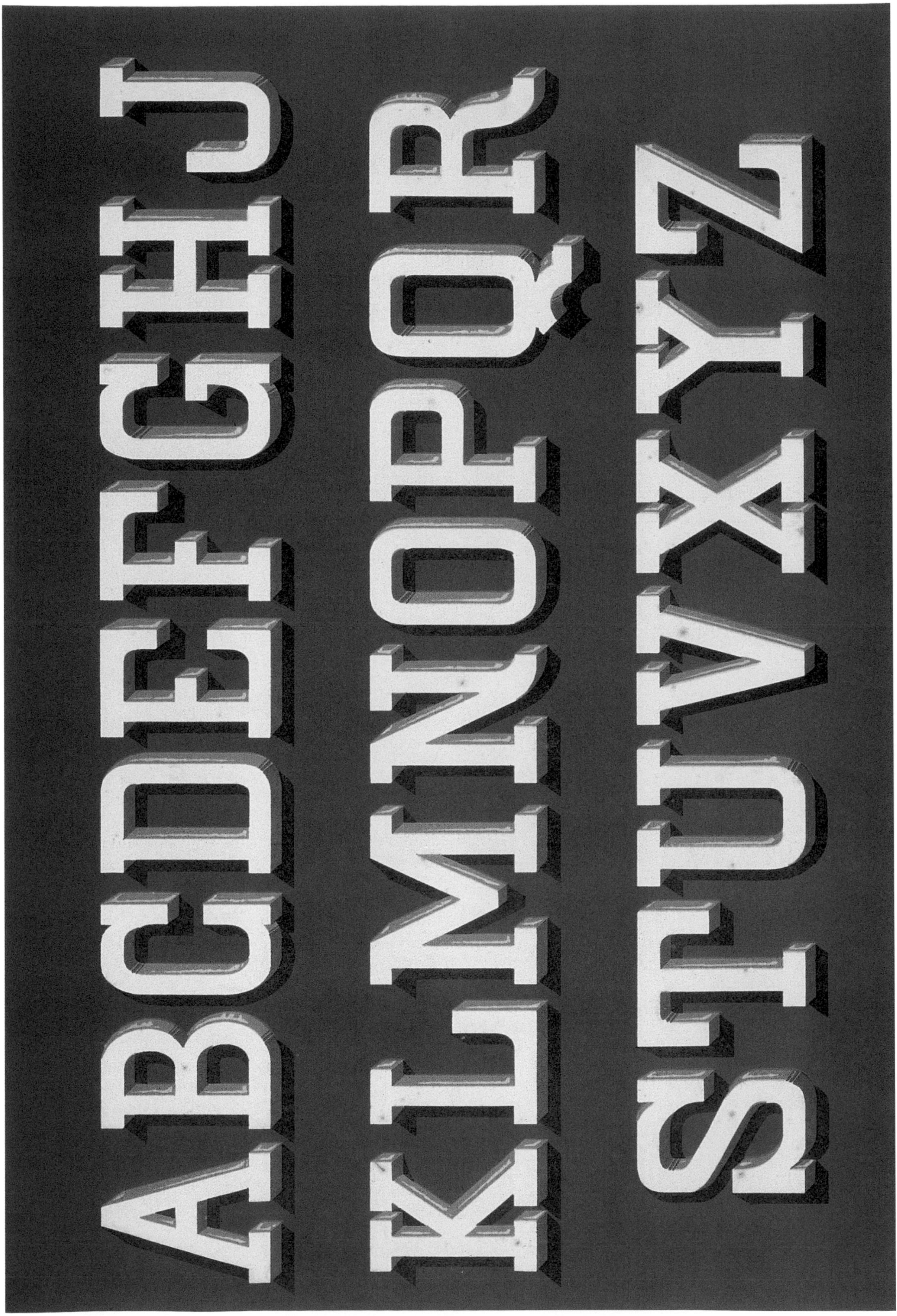

ABCDEFGHIJ
KLMNOPQR
STUVWXYZ

BIER TRINK STUBE

TELEPHON

I.GALERIE

[.STIEGE

BUFFET

KUNST-UND-NATURBLUMEN HANDLUNG

ATELIER

ENTRÉE

WEIN KOST HALLE

RESERVIRT

VERLAG · VON · FRIEDR · WOLFRUM · U · C? · WIEN · U · LEIPZIG

Schmale Jonisch.

ABCDEF
GHIJKLMN
OPQRSTUV
WXYZ

Schriftgiesserei Genzsch & Heyse, Hamburg.

Schattierte Jonisch.

ABCDEFGHI
JKLMNOPQRST
UVWXYZ
abcdefghijklmno
pqrstuvwxyz
1234567890

Schriftgiesserei Flinsch, Frankfurt a. M.

Halbfette Egyptienne.

ABCDEFGHIJ
KLMNOPQRSTU
VWXYZ
abcdefghijklmno
pqrstuvwxyz

Schriftgiesserei Bauer & Comp., Stuttgart.

Breite Egyptienne.

ABCDEFGHIJKLMNO
PQRSTUVWXYZ
abcdefghijklmnopqrstu
vwwxyz
1234567890

Lichte Jonisch.

ABCDE
FGHIJK
LMNOP
QRSTUV
WXYZ

Schriftgiesserei Jul. Klinkhardt, Leipzig.

Kursiv.

ABCDEFGHI
JKLMNOPQRS
TUVWXYZ
abcdefghijklmn
opqrstuvwxyz
1234567890

Schriftgiesserei Schelter & Giesecke, Leipzig.

118

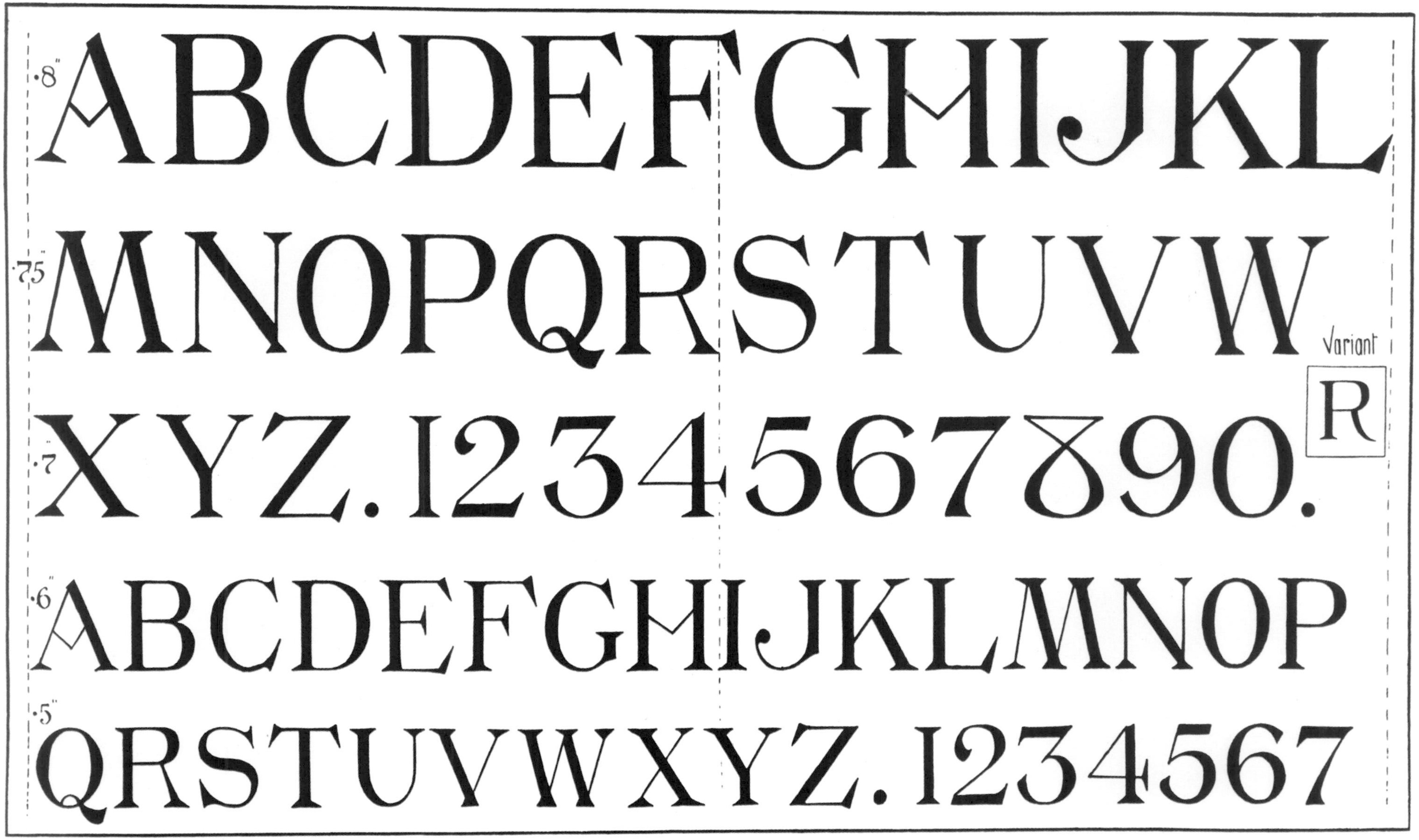

ABCDEFGHIJKL
MNOPQRSTUVW
variant [R]
XYZ.1234567890.

ABCDEFGHIJKL
QRSTUVWXYZ.1234567

Old Roman or Renaissance : Alphabets and Figures.

PLATE 91.

236

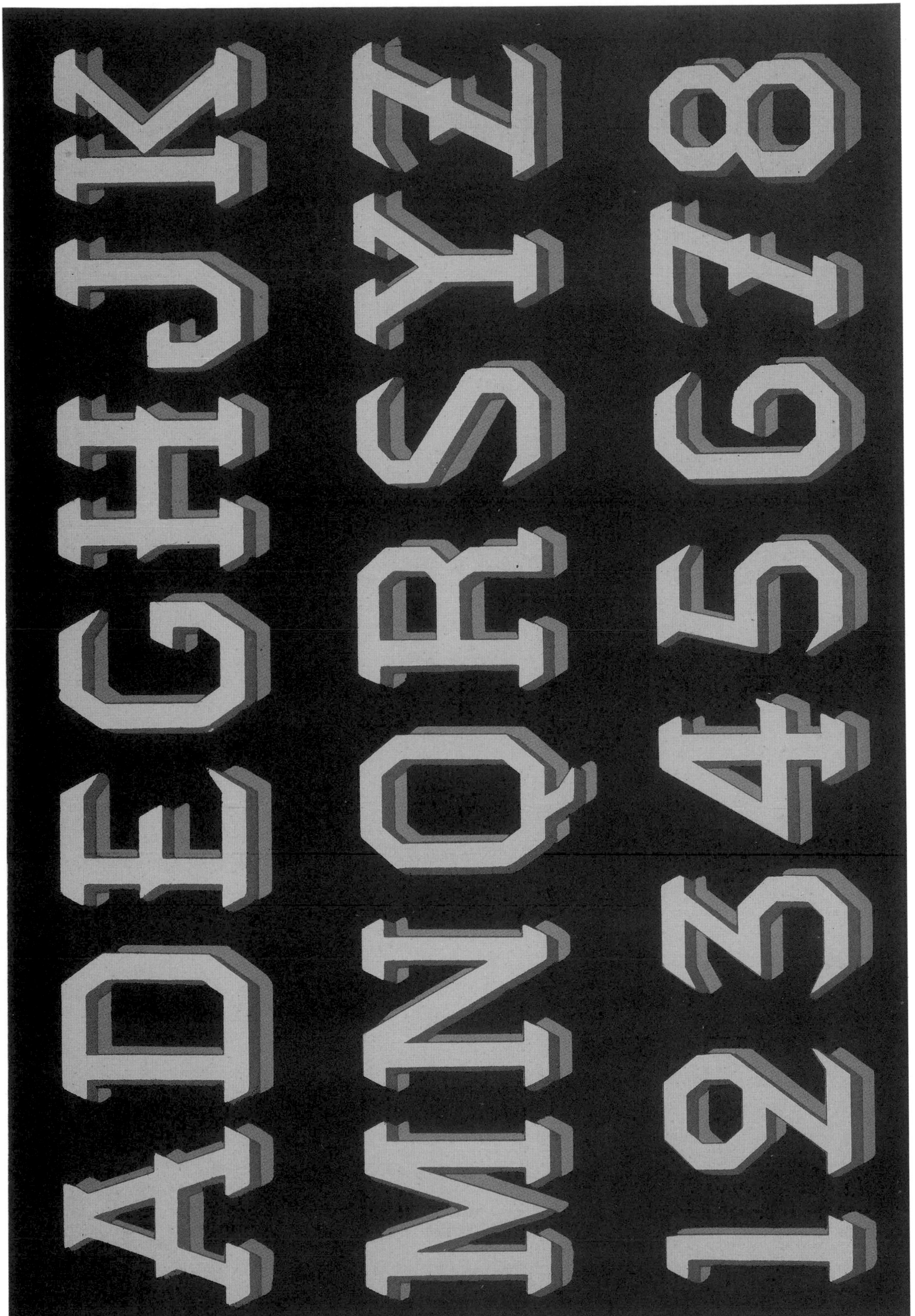
ADEGHJK
MNQRSYZ
12345678

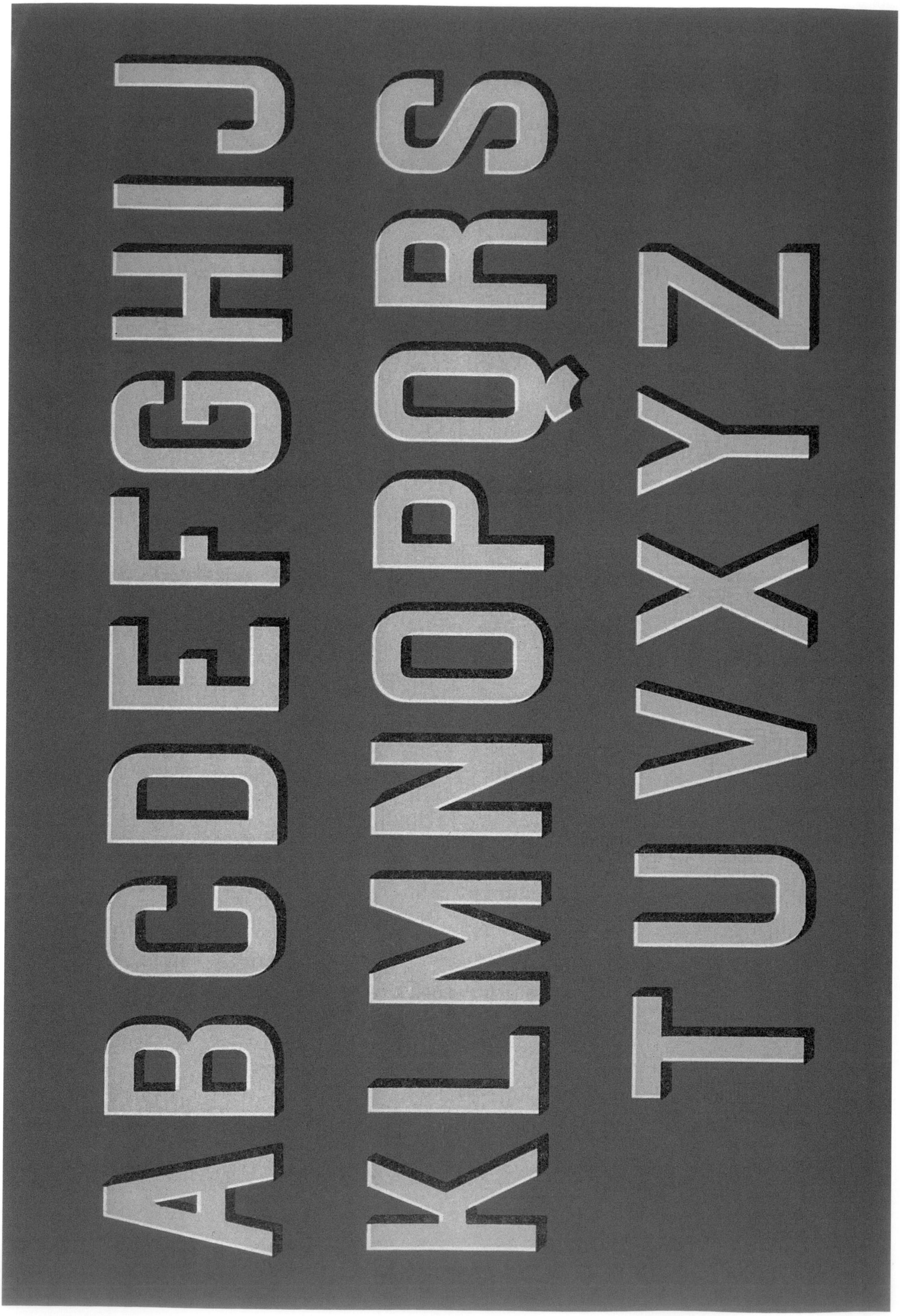

ABCDEFGHIJ
KLMNOPQRS
TUVXYZ

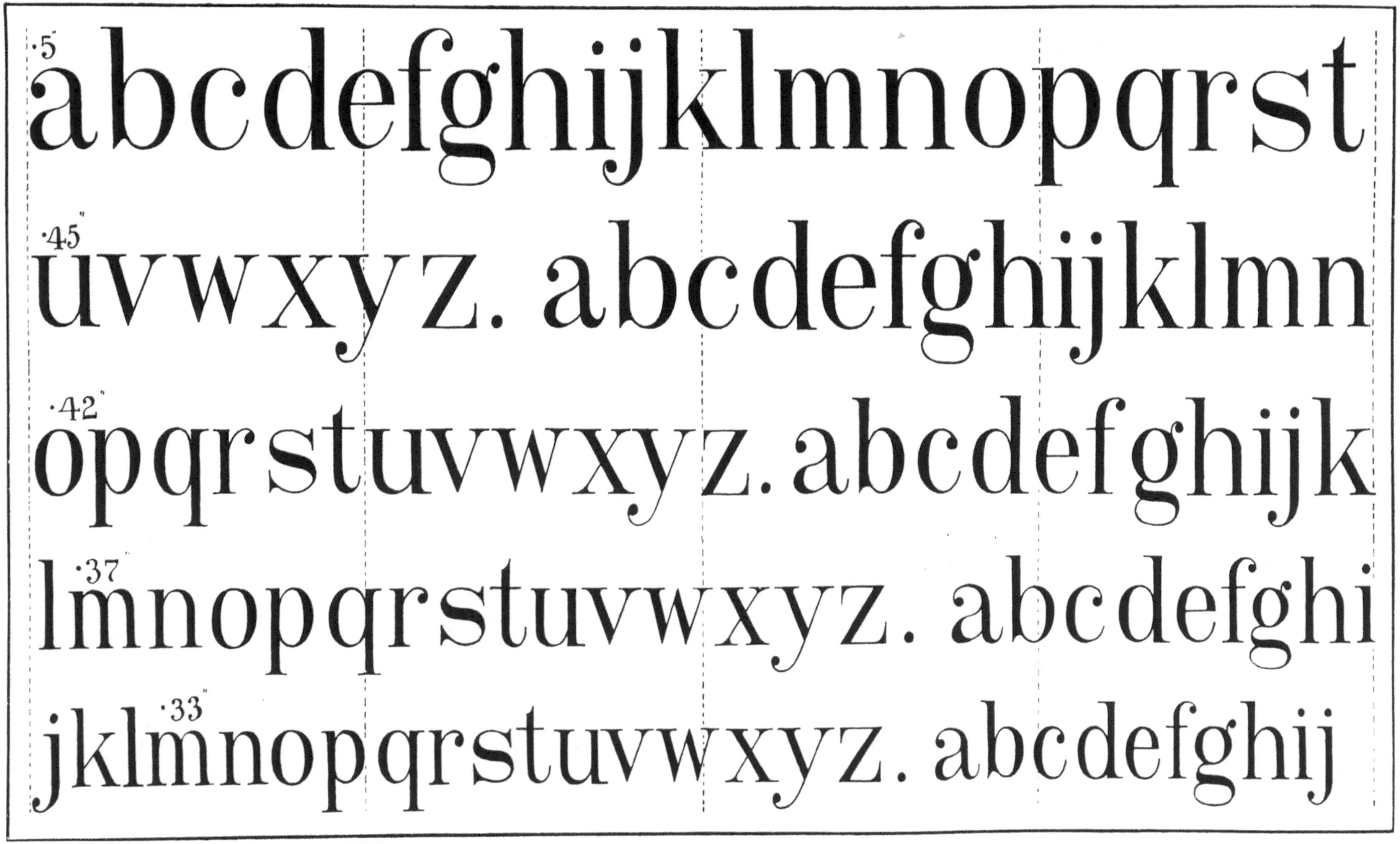

.5 abcdefghijklmnopqrst

.45 uvwxyz. abcdefghijklmn

.42 opqrstuvwxyz. abcdefghijk

1 .37 lmnopqrstuvwxyz. abcdefghi

.33 jklmnopqrstuvwxyz. abcdefghij

Modern Roman Vertical Smalls :   In alphabetical order and correctly spaced :   Ink Exercises.   PLATE 72.

ABCDEFGHIJKLMNOPQRS
TUVWXZ&2234567890.;,Y

abcdefghijklmnopqrstuvwxyz.–

ABCDEFGHIJKLMNOPQR
STUWXYZ&I234567890

abcdefghijklmnopqrstuvwxyz.V

Thick Block Vertical Capitals, Figures, and Smalls:
Thick Block Vertical Capitals, Figures, and Smalls, Serif-relieved:

In alphabetical order and correctly spaced.   PLATE

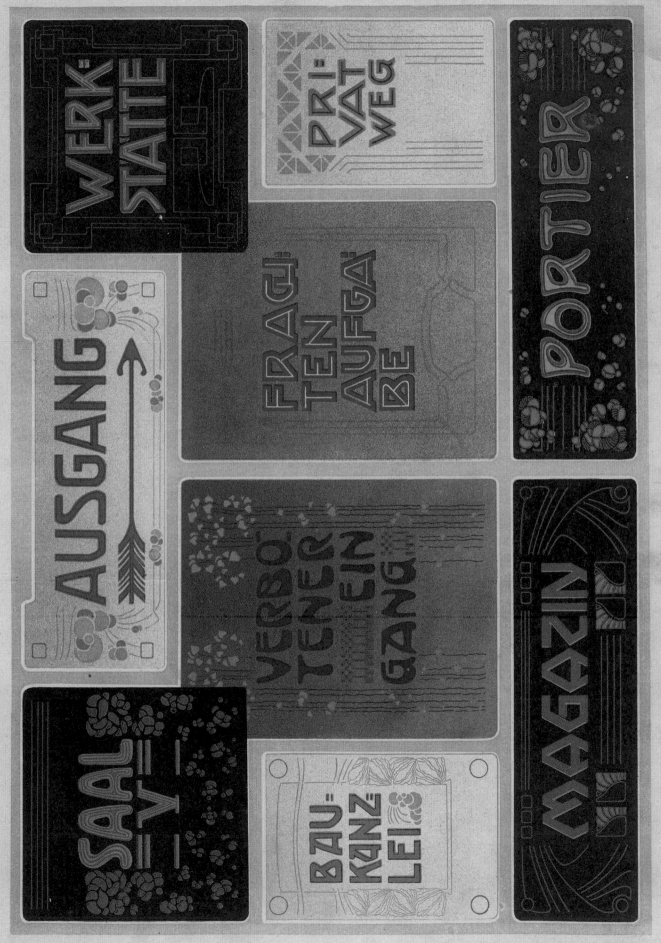

WERK-STÄTTE

PRI-VAT WEG

PORTIER

AUSGANG

FRAG- TEN AUFGA- BE

VERBO- TENER EIN GANG

SAAL V

BAU- KANZ LEI

MAGAZIN

VERLAG · VON · FRIEDR · WOLFRUM · U · C° · WIEN · U · LEIPZIG

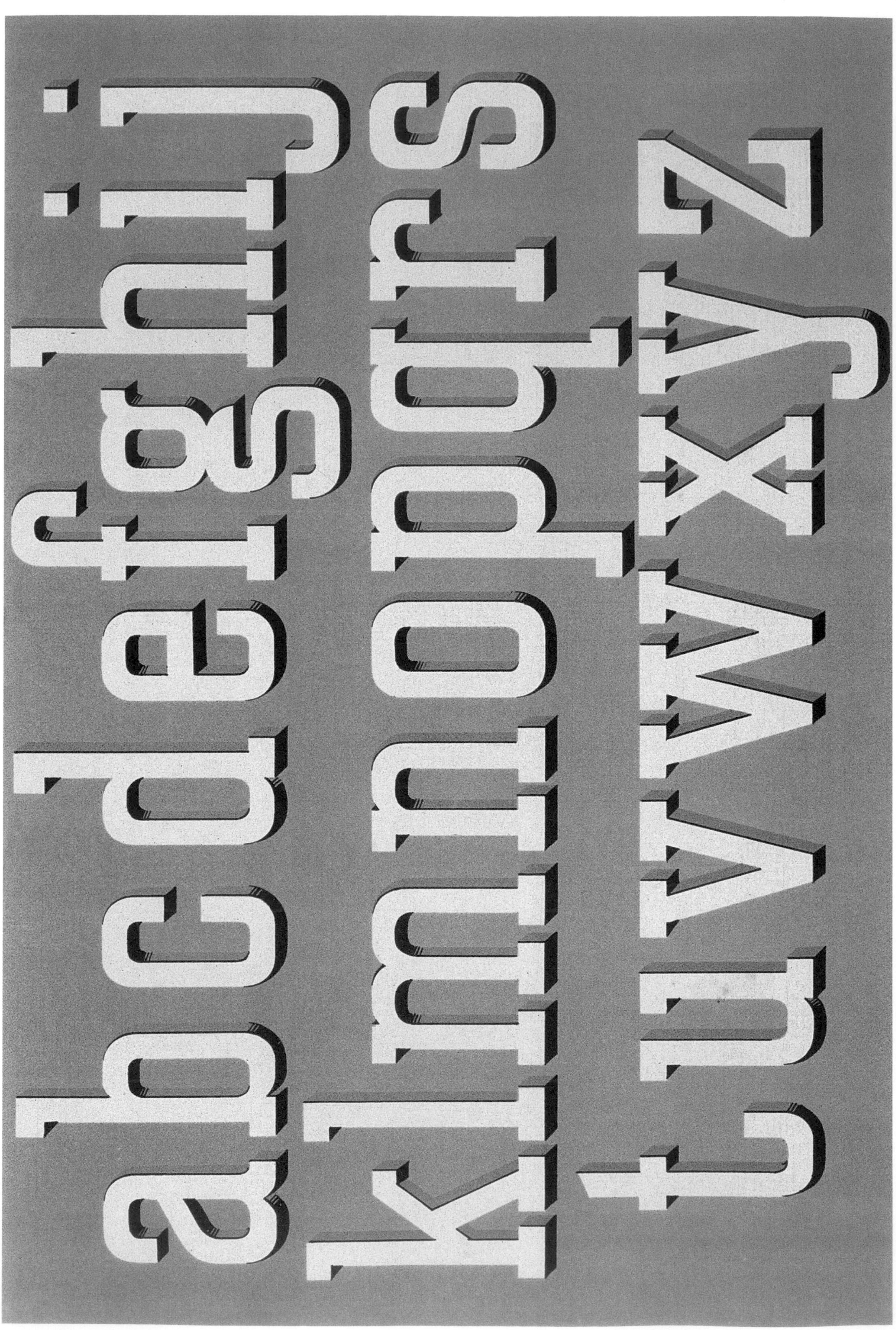

abcdefghij
klmnopqrs
tuvwxyz

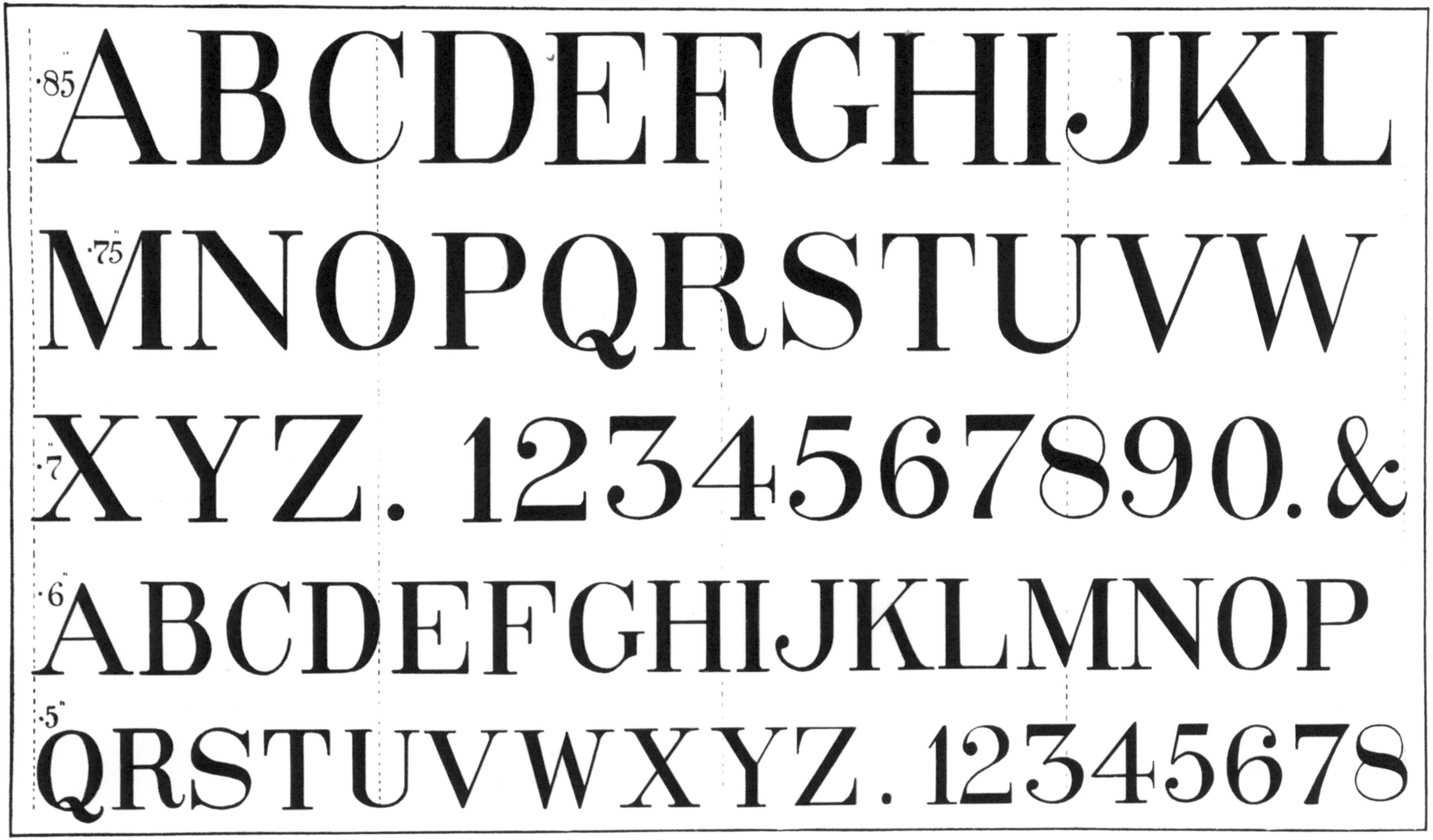

ABCDEFGHIJKL
MNOPQRSTUVW
XYZ.1234567890.&
ABCDEFGHIJKL
QRSTUVWXYZ.1234567

Modern Roman Vertical Capitals: Alphabetically and numerically arranged, and correctly spaced: Ink.   PLATE 67.

{ abcdefghijklmnopq }

{ rstuvwxyz. abcdefghi }

68°

1234567890.1234

567890.1234567890.12

34567890.1234567890.12

Modern Roman Italic Figures :   In numerical order and correctly spaced :   Pencil and Ink Exercises.   PLATE 4.

244

abcdefghij
klmnopqr
stuvxyz

MONROCQ FRÈRES, ÉDITEURS, 3, RUE SUGER, PARIS.

L. RAMADE, PINX.

COIFFEUR

PAPETERIE
LIBRAIRIE F. BOUDIER JOURNAUX

DÉMÉNAGEMENTS

ABCDEFGHIJKLMN
OPQRSTUVWXYZ&

ABCDEFGHIJKLMN
OPQRSTUVWXYZ&

.65

.65

23456789.23456789.

PLATE 103.

Showing mode of hand-finishing where underlined.

Use of Stencils:

247

Breite (geschweifte) Italienne.

A B C D E F G H I J K L M N O P Q R S T U V W X Y Z 1 2 3 4 5 6 7 8 9 0

Schriftgiesserei von Genzsch & Heyse in Hamburg.

Italienne Kursiv.

A B C D E F G H I J K L M N O P Q R S T U V W X Y Z
a b c d e f g h i j k l m n o p q r s t u v w x y z
1 2 3 4 5 6 7 8 9 0

Schriftgiesserei von Schelter & Giesecke in Leipzig.

Schattierte Italienne.

A B C D E F G H I J K L M N O P Q R S T U V W X Y Z
a b c d e f g h i j k l m n o p q r s t u v w x y z

Schriftgiesserei Flinsch in Frankfurt a. M.

Italienne.

A B C D E F G H I J K L M N O P Q R S T U V W X Y Z 1 2 3 4 5 6 7 8 9 0

Schriftgiesserei von Genzsch & Heyse in Hamburg.

Italienne Kursiv.

A B C D E F G H I J K L M N O P Q R S T U V W X Y Z

Schriftgiesserei von Julius Klinkhardt in Leipzig.

Breite Italienne.

A B C D E F G H I J K L M N O P Q R S T U V W X Y Z
a b c d e f g h i j k l m n o p q r s t u v w x y z 1 2 3 4 5 6 7 8 9 0

Schriftgiesserei von Schelter & Giesecke in Leipzig.

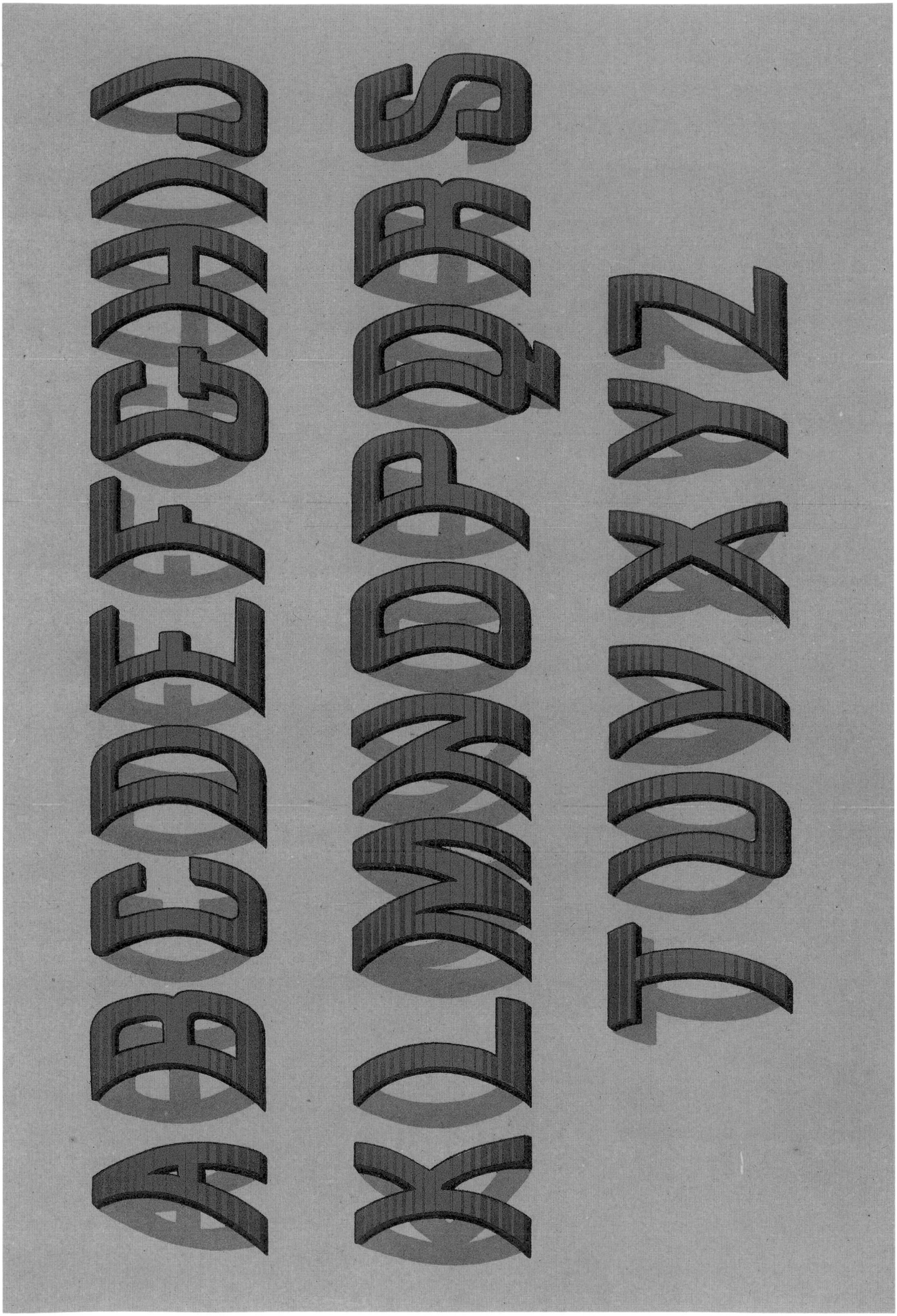

ABCDEFGHIJ
KLMNOPQRS
TUVWXYZ

abcdef
ghijklm
nopqrs
tuvxyz
1234567890.&

le mot.

N° 3. — 1re Année   10 Centimes   Samedi 19 Déc. 1914.

dans ce numéro

LE KRONPRINZ

par

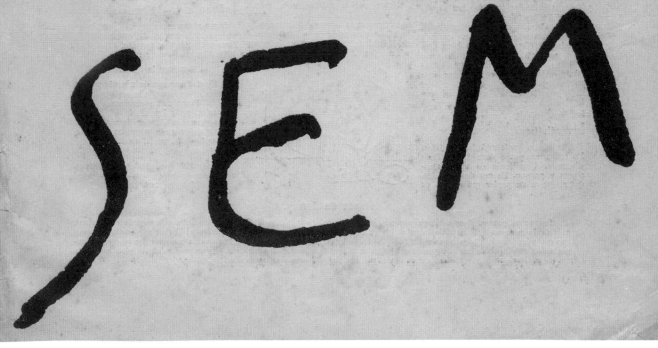

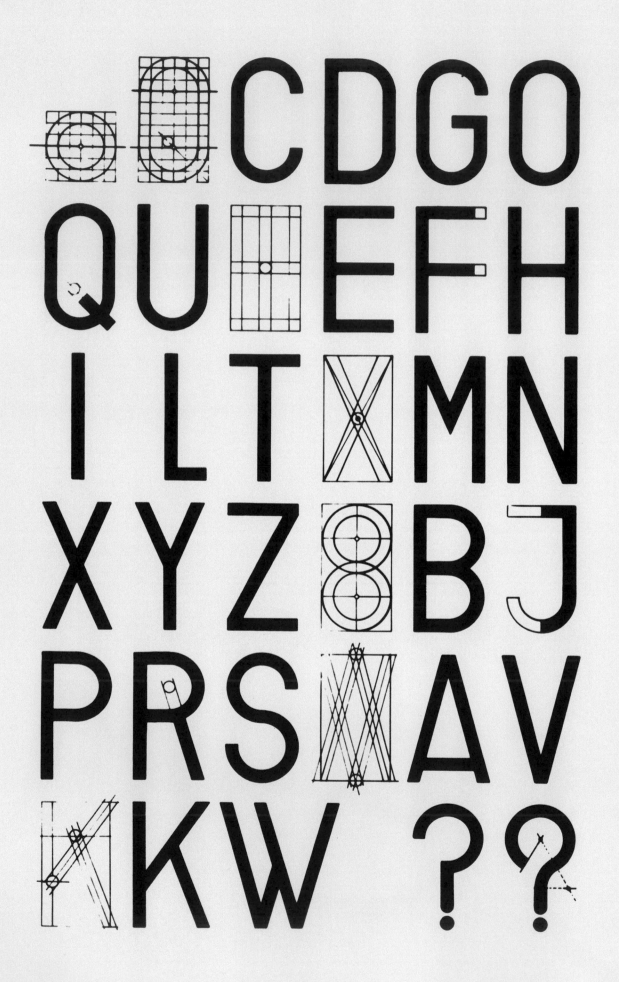

1o DE MAYO
1946

EN DEFENSA DEL PROGRESO SOCIAL DE MEXICO   CINCUENTA CENTAVOS

LOS

JUDAS

DEL

MEXICO

DE

HOY

CUANDO TRUENEN ESTOS JUDAS
NO QUEDARA NI EL MECATE

ABCDE
FGHIJK
LMNOP
QRSTU
VWXYZ
&$!?&&
12345
67890

SEGUNDO PRÉMIO

VENDIDO PELA FELIZ CASA

TESTA

61585

12.000 CONTOS

NA LOTARIA
DE 27 DE OUTUBRO DE 1989

NÃO ESQUEÇA...
SE QUER FESTA JOGUE NO TESTA

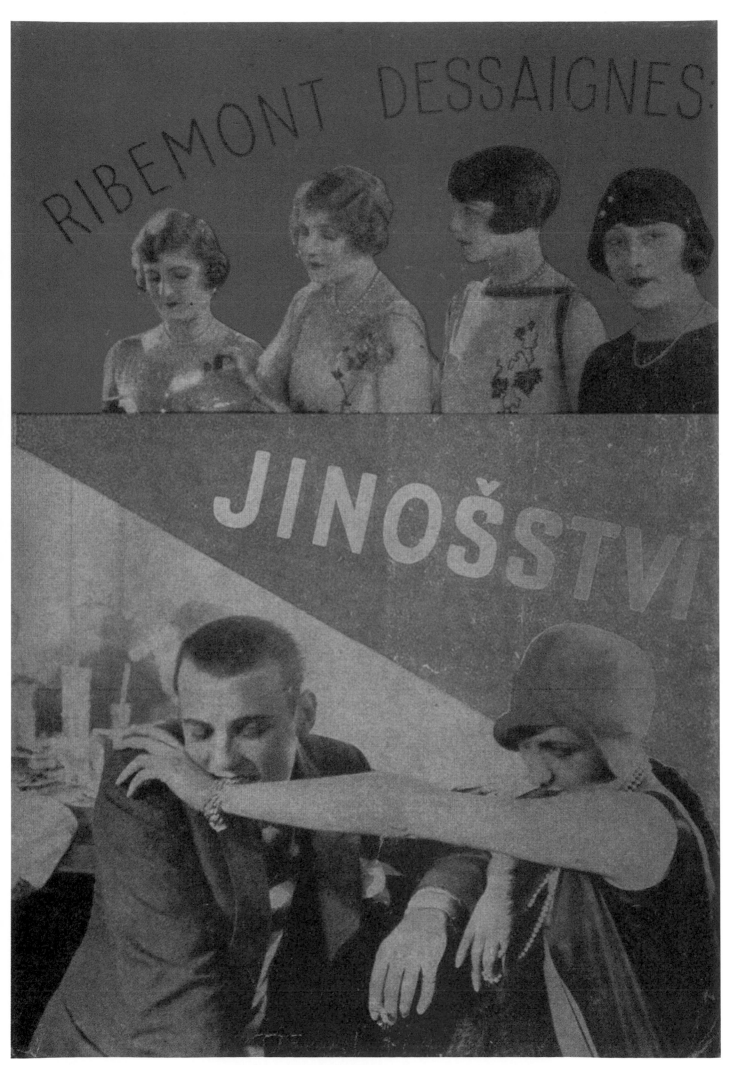

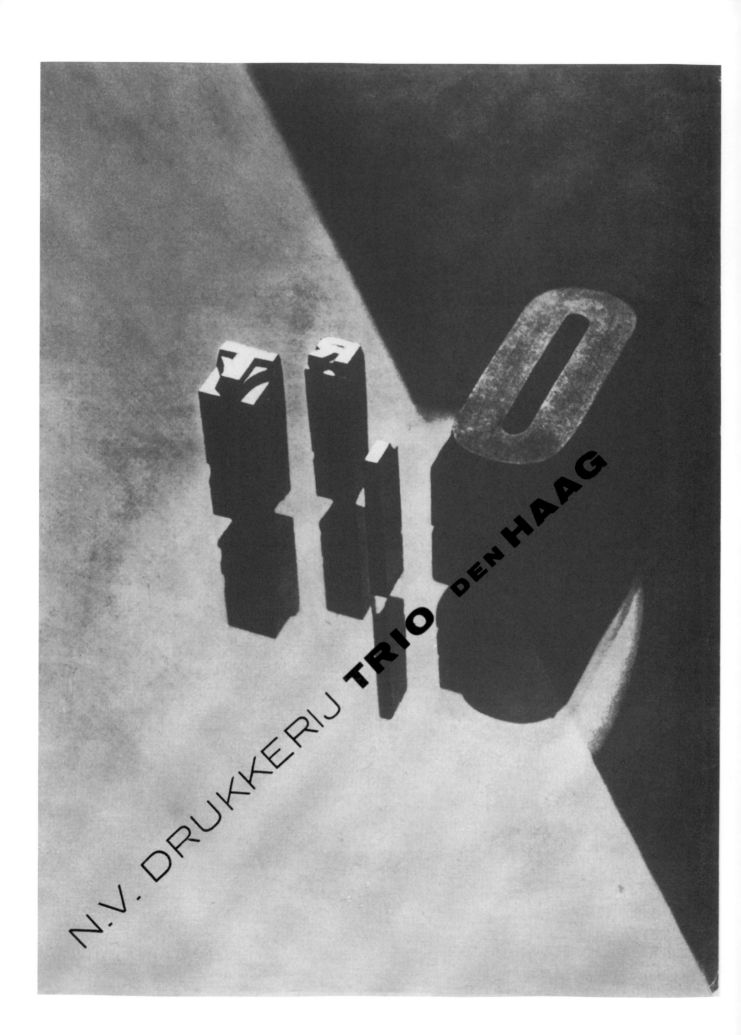

De juiste plaatsing van het adres

op de envelop is van veel belang.

Het adres mag niet alle ruimte in beslag nemen, er moet plaats blijven voor postzegels en voor dienstaanwijzingen, b.v. per luchtpost, aanteekenen, aangegeven waarde. En er moet ook nog plaats blijven voor de naam van den afzender, een firmanaam of een reclame.

Om alles netjes op de juiste plaats te krijgen deel je de envelop het beste zóó in ☞

De bovenste 4 cm moet je **vrij houden** voor postzegels en voor dienstaanwijzingen: de postzegels rechts, de dienstaanwijzingen links.

Van wat onder deze strook overblijft is het rechter gedeelte (**a**) ter breedte van ongeveer **11 cm** voor het **adres**.

In het linker strookje (**b**) kan het adres van den afzender komen of een firmanaam of een reclame.

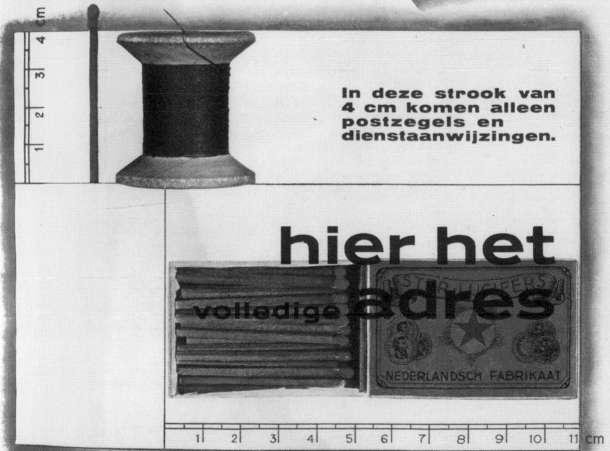

In deze strook van 4 cm komen alleen postzegels en dienstaanwijzingen.

hier het volledige adres

Behalve vakje **b** is ook de achterkant van een envelop een uitstekende plaats om er je eigen adres **te schrijven**, natuurlijk goed leesbaar en volledig. Als je brief soms niet besteld kan worden, b.v. omdat de geadresseerde op reis is, dan kan de post de brief altijd aan je terugbezorgen.

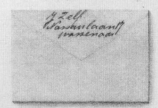

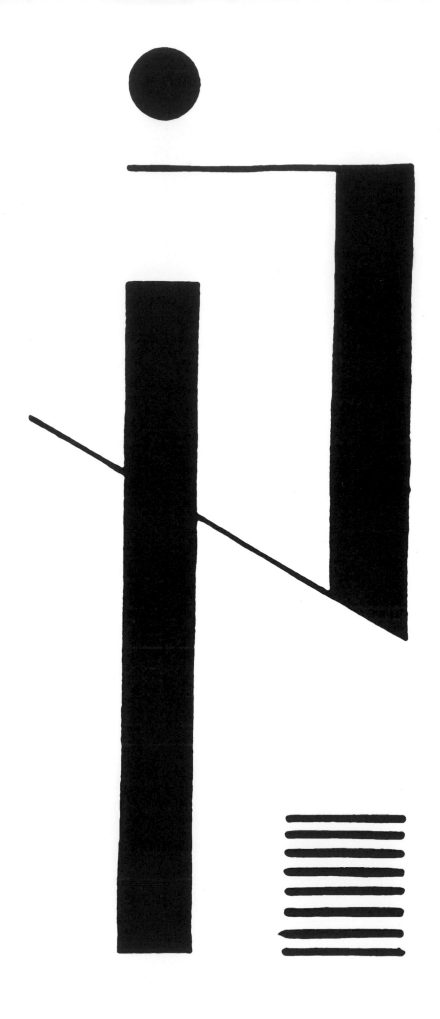

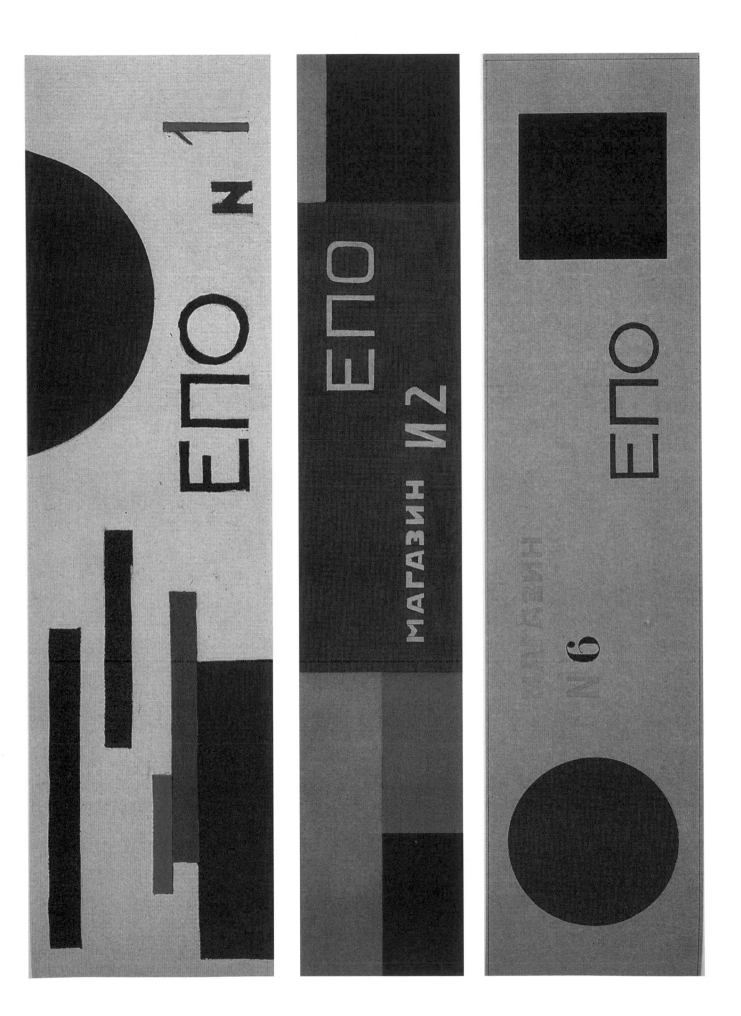

Betracht, und so wird auch für die elementare Typographie meist die Groteskschrift verwendet, weil sie das Ursprüngliche in der Schrift am meisten verkörpert und ohne persönliche Merkmale ist. Hier bei dieser Karte aber wurde die Neuland-Type verwendet, ohne störend zu wirken. Mit solchen Experimenten heisst es aber vorsichtig sein. **B** Was soll denn nun aus den vielen anderen schönen Schriften werden, wenn wirklich die neue Kunst um sich greift? **A** Bisher haben die Groteskschriften ungestört in der Ecke gelegen, und nun werden sie eben mal dran kommen. Ist das nicht ein gerechter Ausgleich? **B** Ach, darum ist wohl der Text der Beilage auch gleich so gesetzt, ich meine in Grotesk. Vielleicht gar aus Sympathie? — **A** O, Sie alter Zyniker! Hier kam es doch auf eine ruhige, möglichst kräftige Type an, welche die Beispiele gut hervortreten lässt. **B** Na, klotzig genug sieht sie auch aus. **A** Aber gut in der Flächenwirkung. Wie gefällt Ihnen denn die Aufmachung dieser Beilage in der neuen Art? Jedenfalls ein Mittelweg, der auch für Prospekte usw. gut geeignet wäre. **B** Nun ja, aber ich weiss nicht, hübsch ist anders. **A** Ich finde gerade, dass sich die Seiten mit den Ecken ganz gut ausnehmen. Es liegt Abwechslung darin. **B** Ja, im Fahrten- und Abenteuerbuch liegt auch Abwechslung, ein Bild so und eins so. Ich kann nicht sagen, dass das „sachlich" ist. **A** Freilich hatte auch ich mir gedacht, dass Tschichold andere Wege der Buchkunst finden würde. Vielleicht hat er sich bewusst bezähmt; vielleicht hat auch die Büchergilde ein Wort mitgesprochen. **B** Die werden sowieso am Umsatz der Bücher den „Erfolg" (?) merken! **A** Sie meinen wohl, dass durch die neue Ausstattung die Zahl der Mitglieder steigt? **B** Das wollen wir erst mal sehen! **A** Nun hören Sie mal. Falls Sie auch Lust haben sollten, sich mal in Konstruktivismus zu versuchen, will ich Ihnen ein paar Thesen mit auf den Weg geben: I. Typographie kann unter Umständen Kunst sein. II. Gestaltung ist Wesen aller Kunst, die typographische Gestaltung ist nicht Abmalen des textlichen Inhalts. III. Auch die nichtbedruckten Stellen sind positive Werte. IV. Qualität der Type bedeutet Einfachheit und Schönheit. Die Einfachheit schliesst in sich Klarheit, eindeutige, zweckentsprechende Form, Verzicht auf allen entbehrlichen Ballast. Schönheit bedeutet gutes Ausbalancieren der Fläche. Die Forderung an die Typographie ist — **B** Hören Sie auf, mir wird ganz schlecht! **A** Schön! Für heute wollen wir dieses Thema abbrechen, beherzigen Sie meine Worte und verwerten Sie das Gute des „Elementaren".

B Eigentlich war es überhaupt Unfug, sich darüber noch lange zu unterhalten und vier Seiten kostbares Papier zu vergeuden, denn wir stehen ja heute mitten im Konstruktivismus, und es wird nicht lange dauern, bis auch diese Sensation ihr Ende gefunden hat. Denn so war's und ist's noch in der Welt: Im steten Wechsel liegt ja der Reiz des Lebens. **A** Ei, Donnerwetter, Sie sprechen ja so geistreich und verständig! — Gewiss vereinbart sich nicht alles im Konstruktivismus mit unseren bisherigen Anschauungen über Typographie, aber die für ihn erbrachten Begründungen sind nicht ohne weiteres von der Hand zu weisen. Der grösste Teil seiner Widersacher stützt sich meistens auf unbestimmte Gefühle. Wollen wir doch froh sein, dass wir aus der „elementaren typographie" neue Anregungen und Gedanken gewonnen haben, die leider oft in ganz falscher Verkennung der inneren Zusammenhänge weidlich ausgenutzt werden und so bei dem kritischen Beschauer ein nicht immer befriedigendes Gefühl auslösen. **B** Jedenfalls hat man um die neue Art Satzgruppierung, die man plötzlich mit „Kunst" bezeichnet, viel zuviel Wesens gemacht. Drum sei auch der Debatte ein Punkt gesetzt.

T

BERATUNGEN
UND ENTWÜRFE
WERBEDRUCKE

GEORG KLEMM
NICOLAISTR. 22
FERNRUF 35308

REKLAME
DRESDEN—A. 16

GESCHÄFTSKARTE ENTWURF HANS MENKE DRESDEN

GEBRAUCHSGRAPHIK

HEFT:

1. JAHR

1924/25

1/7

"DAS BÜRO"

MONATSSCHRIFT ZUR FÖRDERUNG KÜNSTLERISCHER REKLAME

PHÖNIX DRUCK UND VERLAG G.M.B.H. BERLIN SW 68

HDK

Таб. I.   К Проблеме Композиции:

К.Клюн 1942 г.

266

A A B b C c D d E e F f G g

H h I i J j K k L l M m N n

O o P p Q q R r S s T t U u

V v W w X x Y y Z z

1 2 3 4 5 6 7 8 9 0

1 2 3 4 5 6 7 8 9 0

ABCDE
FGHIJK
LŁMNO
PRSTU
oWYŻo
* 1234567890 *

JUGEZ LA VALEUR DE NOS SERVICES· PAR DEUX FAITS PRÉCIS

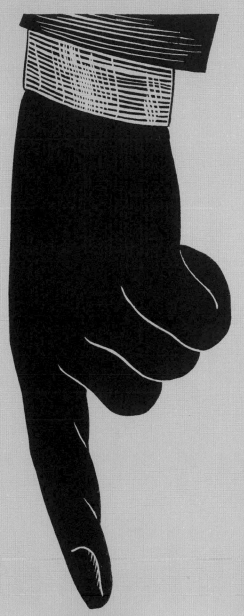

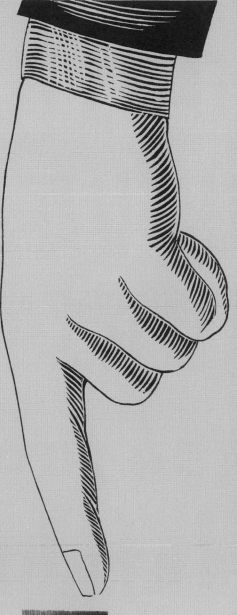

EDITIONS **PAUL·MARTIAL** PARIS

MAQUETTES **DEVIS**
PREPARÉS GRATUITEMENT

AFFICHES

CATALOGUES

DÉPLIANTS

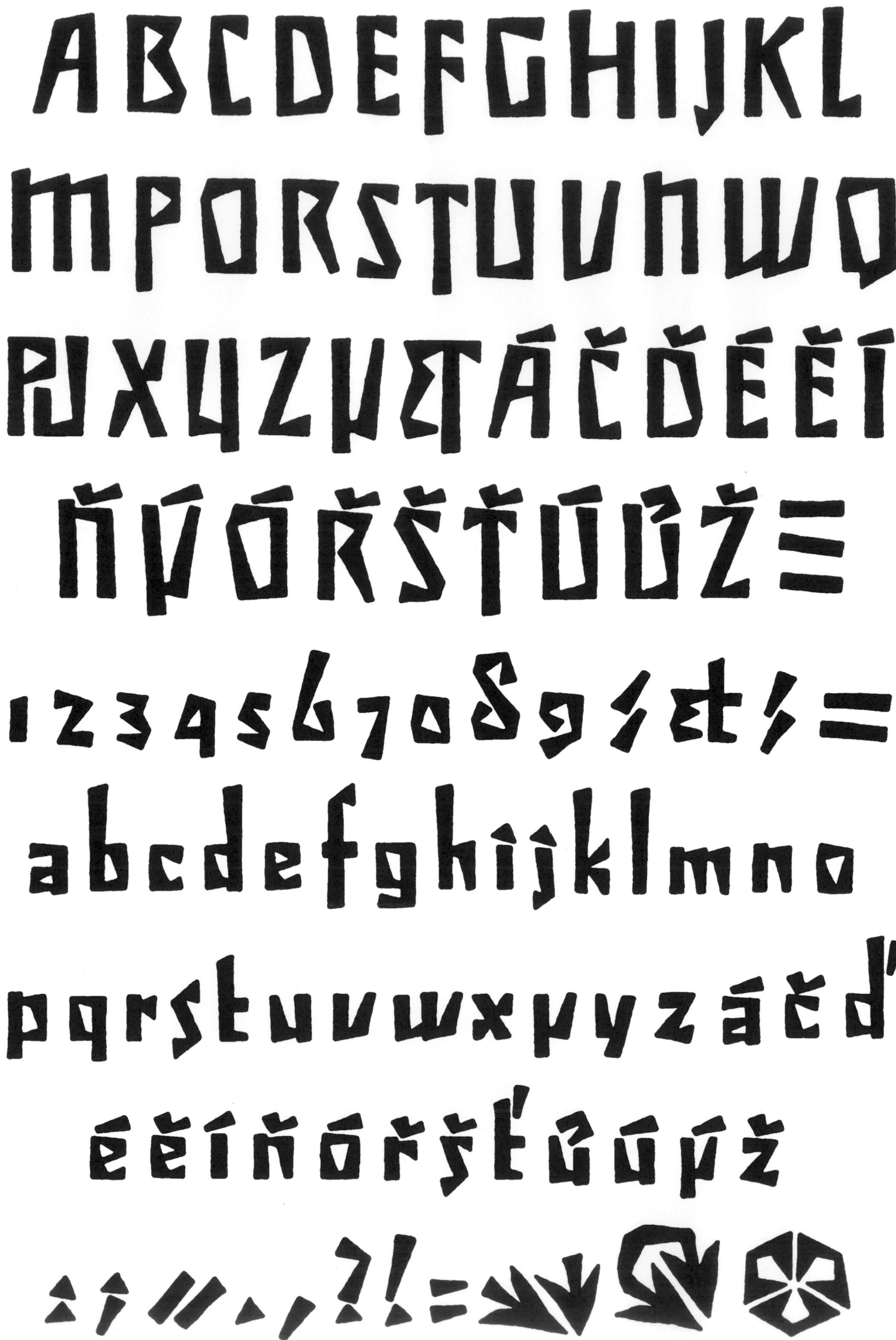

ABCDEFGHIJKL

MPQRSTUUVNWO

PRXYZVßÁČČĎÉĚÍ

ŇÚÓŘŠŤŮÓŽ≡

1234567oðgzεtz=

abcdefghijklmno

pqrstuuvwxpyzáčďď

ěěíňñořšťžůópž

⸳⸳⸳⸳,?!⸳⸺→⟲⬡

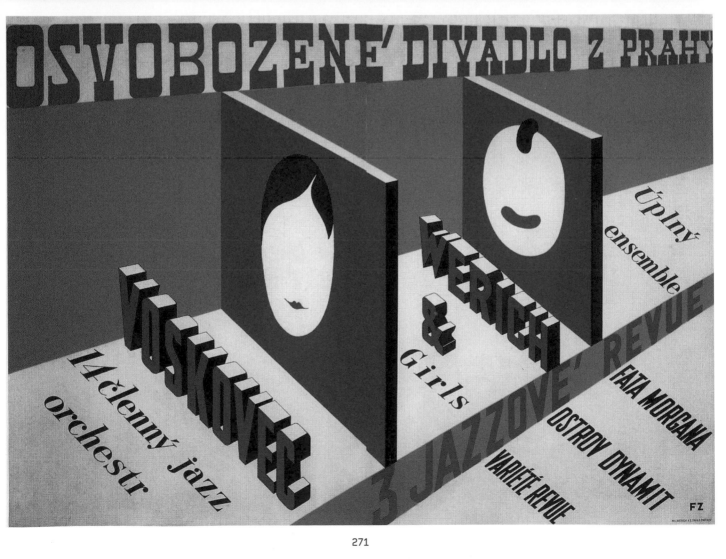

PADILLA,
EN LUCHA ELECTORAL

PADILLA,
TAL COMO ES

А Б В Г Д
Е Ж З И К
Л М Н О П
Р С Т У Ф Х
Ц Ч Щ Щ Я
1 2 3 4 5 6 7 8 9 0
ГАЗЕТА

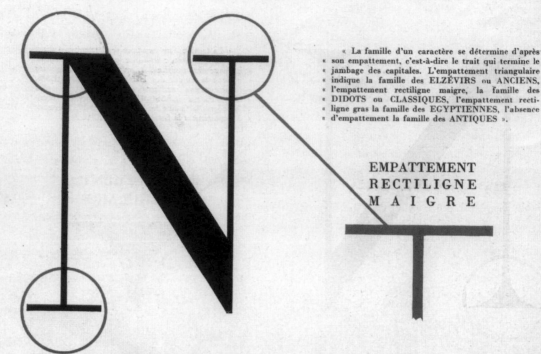

« La famille d'un caractère se détermine d'après son empattement, c'est-à-dire le trait qui termine le jambage des capitales. L'empattement triangulaire indique la famille des ELZÉVIRS ou ANCIENS, l'empattement rectiligne maigre, la famille des DIDOTS ou CLASSIQUES, l'empattement rectiligne gras la famille des EGYPTIENNES, l'absence d'empattement la famille des ANTIQUES ».

EMPATTEMENT
RECTILIGNE
MAIGRE

ABCDEFGHIJKLM
NOPQRSTUVWXYZ
abcdefghijklmnopqrstuvwxyz
ABCDEFGHIJKLM
NOPQRSTUVWXYZ
abcdefghijklmnopqrstuvwxyz
1 2 3 4 5   6 7 8 9 0

TYPE DE DIDOT OU CLASSIQUE : LE BODONI

L'ART DE RECONNAITRE UN CARACTÈRE
(PRINCIPE DE THIBAUDEAU)

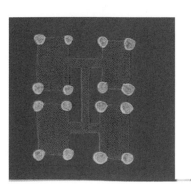   

JAPANESE PAPER. KIMONOS. EXOTIC. DINNERWARE OLD. ORIENTAL KITES TIES FISH

天回來他若今天不來呢那怎麼樣〇有人說山西反了〇這個事情

CHINESE IS BEST SEE LEFT TO RIGHT, BUT VERTICAL READING IS QUITE AUTHENTIC

ABCDEEFGHH
IIJJKLLMNNO
PQRSS TUV
WXYZ 1234567890

mauo

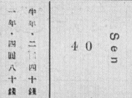

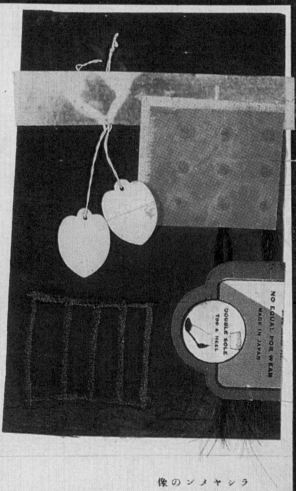

ラシヤメンの像

高見澤路直

Sen
40

LE RELIGIONI NEL MONDO
(1936)

 CRISTIANI    MAOMETTANI    CULTI PRIMIT.   INDUISTI    BUDDISTI CONFU-CIANISTI E SCINTOISTI   ATEI

 BIANCHI   NEGRI    INDO-ATLANTICI   GIALLI

OGNI FIGÜRA : CENTO MILIONI DI UOMINI

Tav. 190

ABCD
EFGHIJK
LMNOPQ
RSTUVX
YZWÇÆ
Œ &

abcdefghi
jklmnopqr
stuvxyzw
çæœfififf

.,;:;'-!?()

CAMPO GRAFICO

RIVISTA DI ESTETICA E DI TECNICA GRAFICA · MILANO · NUMERO 1 · GENNAIO 1939 · SPEDIZ. IN ABBON. POSTALE

ABCDEFGHIJKL
MNOPQRSTUV
WXYZ&.,-'::!?
$1234567890

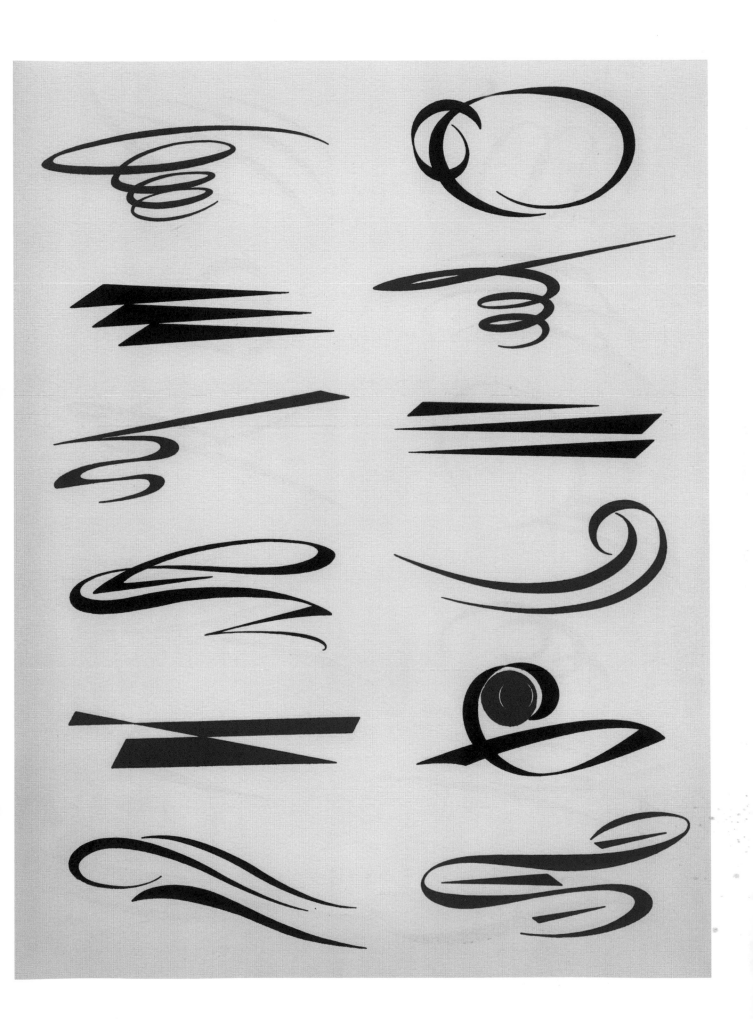

CEREALI E SEMI DA PRATO

КЛАСИЦИСТИЧНА АНТИКВА

А Б В Г Д Е

Ж З И Й К Л М

Н О П Р С Т У

Ф Х Ц Ч Ш Щ

Ъ Ь Ю Я

1 2 3 4 5 6 7 8 9 0

МА́КОВЕЦ

ЖУРНАЛ
ИСКУССТВ

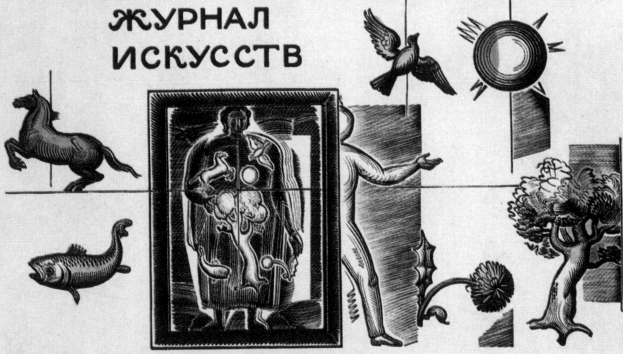

МОСКВА N 3 1923

THE ANTIFASCIST SCHOOLBOOK

In 1937 the republican government of Spain was deeply embroiled in the savage civil war against the fascist rebellion led by General Franco. Under the leadership of the minister of education, Jesús Hernández, the Ministry of Public Information issued *Cartilla Escolar Antifascista*, a literacy primer, as an aid to the campaign of the "cultural militias" against illiteracy. The booklet, beautifully designed by Mauricio Amster, who also created the poster advertising the "schoolbook", combined phonetics with politics, identifying the military struggle against fascism with the cultural fight against ignorance. Pages from this poignant document are reproduced here for the first time since its publication in republican Spain's heroic years of travail and hope. The civil war ended in March 1939, with the final defeat of the republic.

¡VIVA MADRID HEROICO!

VI-VA MA-DRID HE-ROI-CO

Vi-va Ma-drid he-roi-co

i, a, e, o

V, v, M, d, r, h, c

ejercicios: formar otras sílabas, palabras y frases con los elementos ya conocidos.

ejemplos de sílabas:

Ha, he, hi, ho, hu, re, mos, na, Es,
Ha, he, hi, ho, hu, re, mos, na, Es,

As, Is, Os, Us, pa, ña, ñe, fe, fa, fi,
As, Is, Os, Us, pa, ña, ñe, fe, fa, fi,

fo, fu, lir, lar, lur.
fo, fu, lir, lar, lur.

ejemplos de palabras:

Hacer, hago, haces, hacemos, hagamos, haréis, hacían,
Hacer, hago, haces, hacemos, hagamos, haréis, hacían,

hecho, haber, hiena, hierro, honda, hospital, huelga,
hecho, haber, hiena, hierro, honda, hospital, huelga,

Esteban, Ismael, fosa, fusil, feroz.
Esteban, Ismael, fosa, fusil, feroz.

Nuestros combatientes luchan como
Nuestros combatientes luchan como

héroes.
héroes.

JESUS HERNANDEZ, NUESTRO MINISTRO DE INSTRUCCION

Je-sús Her-nán-dez, nues-tro
Mi-nis-tro de Ins-truc-ción.

J-e-s-ú-s H-e-r-n-á-n-d-e-z, n-u-e-s-t-r-o
M-i-n-i-s-t-r-o d-e I-n-s-t-r-u-c-c-i-ó-n.

i, e, u, a, o
J, s, H, r, n, d, z, M, I.

SOLIDARIDAD INTERNACIONAL

So-li-da-ri-dad in-ter-na-cio-nal

o, i, a,

Tra, Tre, Tri, Tro, Tru, ba, be, je,
Tra, Tre, Tri, Tro, Tru, ba, be, je,

ja, ji, jo, ju, mos, mas, pa, pe, ra,
ja, ji, jo, ju, mos, mas, pa, pe, ra,

la, gue, gui, güe, güi, rra, rre.
la, gue, gui, güe, güi, rra, rre.

tropas, ultraje, jovial, agujero, jugo, racimo, ración,
tropas, ultraje, jovial, agujero, jugo, racimo, ración,

trinchera, Trubia, ametralladora, traje, ajetreo, trigo,
trinchera, Trubia, ametralladora, traje, ajetreo, trigo,

barra, rojo, jarra, jara, reloj, aparejo, guijarro,
barra, rojo, jarra, jara, reloj, aparejo, guijarro

pingüe, argüir.
pingüe, argüir,

La juventud gloriosa se bate en
La juventud gloriosa se bate en

las trincheras.
las trincheras.

REPUBLICA DEMOCRATICA

RE-PU-BLI-CA DE-MO-CRA-TI-CA

R-e-p-ú-b-l-i-c-a d-e-m-o-c-r-á-t-i-c-a

e, u, i, a, o

R, p, b, l, c, d, m, r, t

LENIN, NUESTRO GRAN MAESTRO

Le-nin, nues-tro gran ma-es-tro

e, i, u, o, a

L, n, s, t, r, g, m

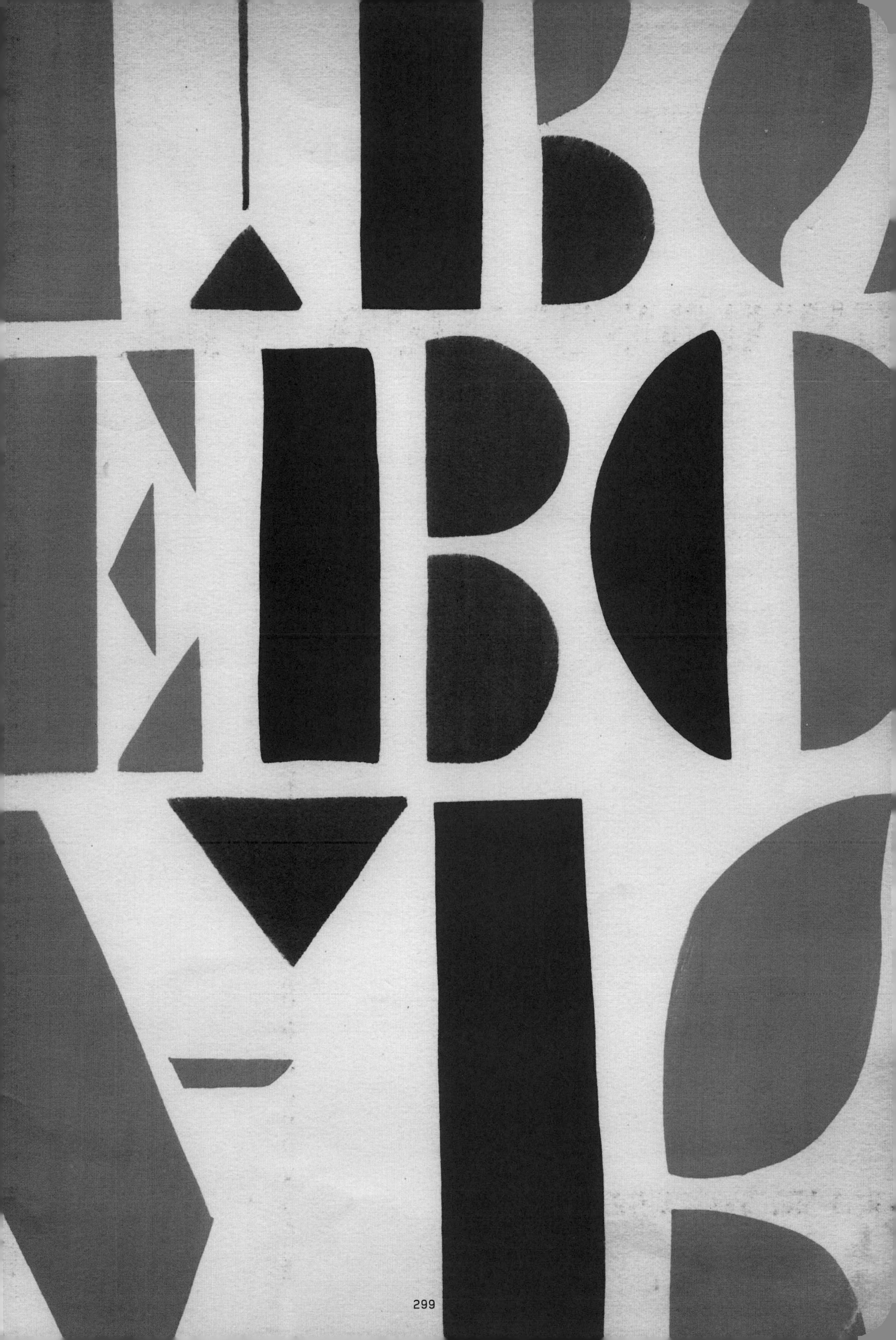

```
ACCIPEPICTANOVISELEGISLVXAVREAMVNDI
CLEMENTISPIASIGNADEIVOTVMQVEPERENNE
SVMMEFAVETETOTAROGATPLEBSGAVDIARITE
ETMERITAMCREDITCVMSERVATIVSSATIMORE
AVGVSTOETFIDEICHRISTISVBLEGEPROBATA
GLORIAIAMSAECLOPROCESSITCANDIDAMITI
ADCVMVLANSCOETVSETTOTAORNATASERENIS
MVNERIBVSPRAESTANSNATISVTLAVREAVOTA
VIRTVTVMTITVLOSPRIMISIAMDEBEATANNIS
PROGENIETALIGENVITQVOSNOBILESAECLVM
HISDECVSAPROAVOETVERAECONSCIAPROLIS
ROMAFLVITPRINCEPSINVICTIMILITISALMA
OTIAPACISAMANSHAECSVNTMITISSIMADONA
HOCATAVIMERITVMVOTISPOSTEDITVSORBIS
ERVMPENSDOCVITNENORINTFRANGEREFIDEI
OPTIMAIVRAPARESCVRISSVBMARTISINIQVI
NVLLISLAESAFIDESHINCIVGISTAMINEFATA
VOBISFILALEGVNTPLACIDAPIETATESECVTA
ETRESCONSTANTINVNCEXERITINCLYTAFAMA
AVCTASTIRPEPIAVOTOACCVMVLATAPERENNI
SANCTATVASSEDESADMENTISGAVDIAMIGRAT
AETHERIORESIDENSFELIXINCARDINEMVNDI
IAMPATRIAEVIRTVTISOPESBELLINELABORE
ANIVSTIMERITISDICAMMENTISQVESERENAE
ETPIADONACANAMFECVNDAQVEPECTORANOTO
RITEDEOSICMENTEVIGENTCVIGAVDIACASTA
CLAVDIVSINVICTVSBELLISINSIGNIAMAGNA
VIRTVTVMTVLERITGOTHICODEMILITEPARTA
FILIAETATEPOTENSCONSTANTIVSOMNIAPACE
ACIVSTISAVCTVSCOMPLERITSAECVLADONIS
HAECPOTIOREFIDEMERITISMAIORIBVSORTA
ORBIDONATVOPRAESTASSVPERASQVEPRIORA
PERQVETVOSNATOSVINCISPRAECONIAMAGNA
ACTIBILEGEDEIIVSSISQVEPERENNIAFIENT
SAECLAPIISCEPTRITECONSTANTINESERENO
```

Elemē-tu.

Nobile faculum.

Roma eluit.

Dicam entiisque faereno

Pilieta-te potens Constan-tinuso-nia

Serena.

F

1

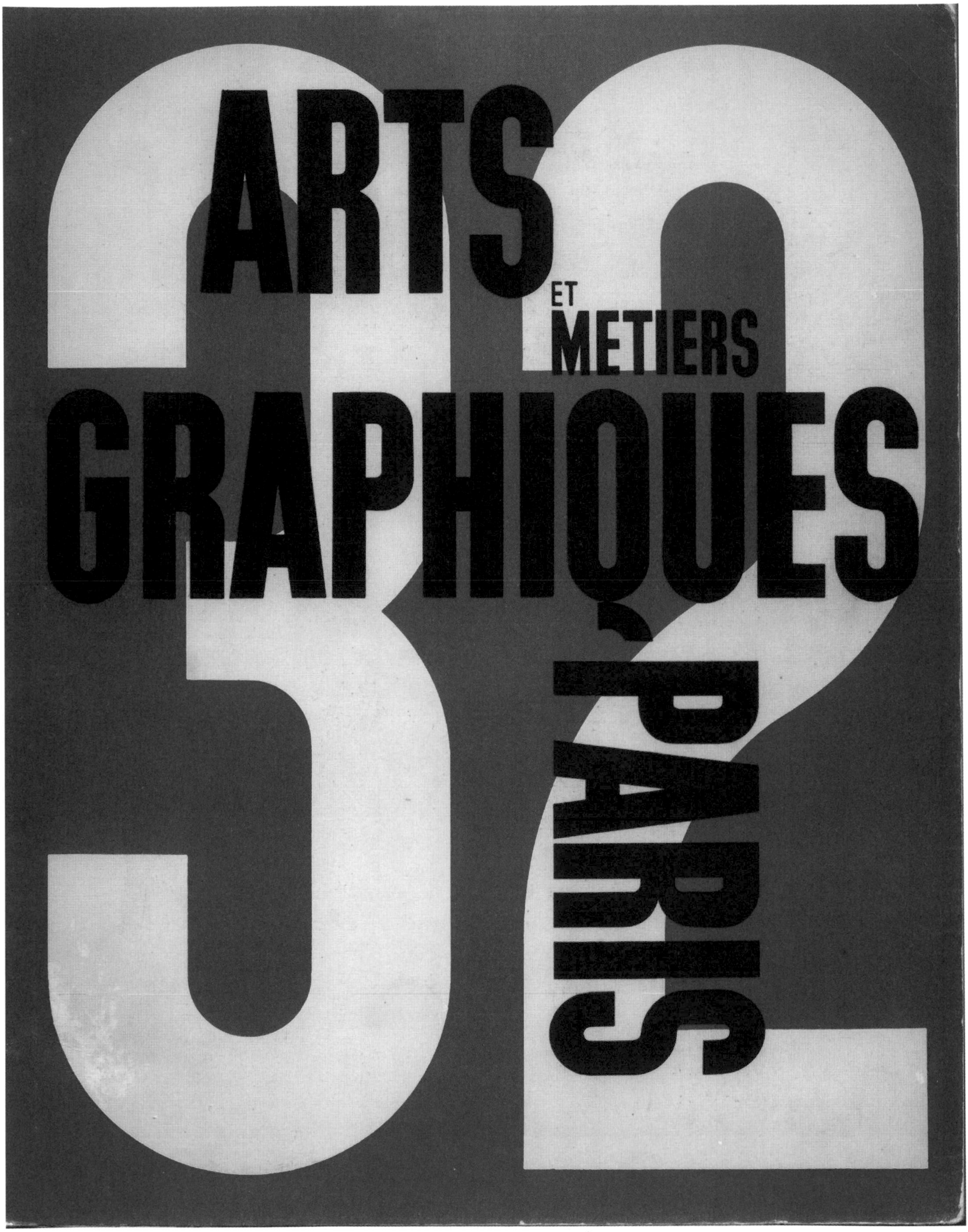

ARTS
ET METIERS
GRAPHIQUES
PARIS
32

Arbeitnehmer in der U.d.S.S.R.

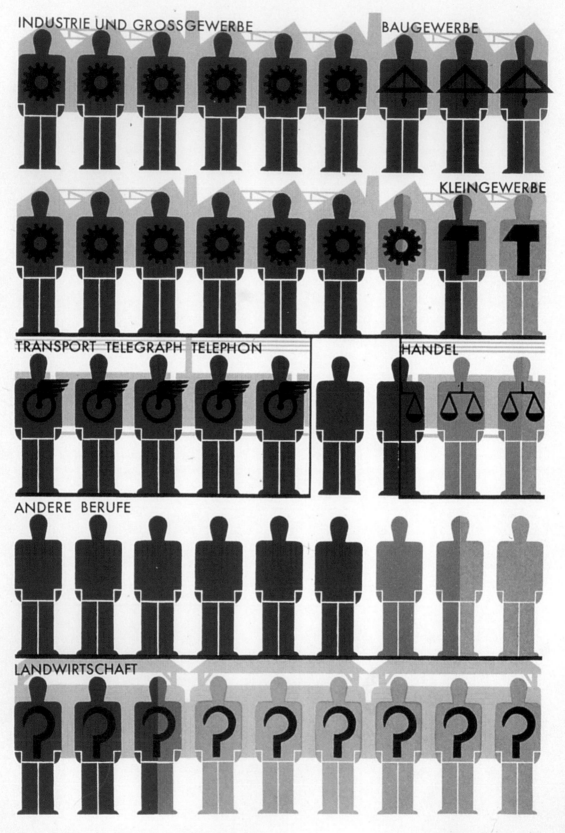

INDUSTRIE UND GROSSGEWERBE

BAUGEWERBE

KLEINGEWERBE

TRANSPORT TELEGRAPH TELEPHON

HANDEL

ANDERE BERUFE

LANDWIRTSCHAFT

Rote Figur 250 000 Arbeitnehmer der Staatswirtschaft
Hellrote Figur 250 000 Arbeitnehmer der Genossenschaften
Blaue Figur 250 000 Arbeitnehmer der Privatwirtschaft
nach „Kontrollziffern des Obersten Wirtschaftsrates" Moskau

Wirtschaftsjahr 1928-29

Angefertigt für das Bibliographische Institut AG., Leipzig
Gesellschafts- und Wirtschaftsmuseum in Wien ©

Gesellschaft und Wirtschaft 86

ABCDEFGHIJ

JKLMNOPQR

STUVWXYZ

aabcdefghi

jklmnopqrsß

tuvwxyz

1234567890

ABCDEFG
HIJKLMN
OPQRST
UVWXYZ
abcdefghij
klmnopqrst
uvwxyzæœ

ARALLELO-
GRAMS

(▮ *and* ▮) *on*
equal baſes, and between the
ſame parallels, are equal.

Draw ▬▬ and ▬ ▬ ▬ ▬ ,

▬ ▬ = ▬▬ = ▬▬ , by (pr. 34, and hyp.) ;

∴ ▬ ▬ = and ‖ ▬▬ ,

∴ ▬▬ ▬ = and ‖ ▬ ▬ ▬ ▬ (pr. 33.)

And therefore ▱ is a parallelogram :

but ▮ = ▰ = ▮ (pr. 35.)

∴ ▮ = ▮ (ax. 1.).

Q. E. D.

4

ABCDEF
GHIJKLM
NOPQRST
UVWXYZ

Rotterdamsche Schilderschool,
A. R. VAN DER BURG

A. R. VAN DER BURG.

6

abcdefghi
jklmnopqrs
tuvwxijyz
1234567890

Rotterdamsche Schilderschool,
A. R. VAN DER BURG

A. R. VAN DER BURG.

ANTIQUE POINTED EXTENDED.

A B C D E F G H I J K
L M N O P Q R S T U V
W X Y Z & .
1 2 3 4 5 6 7 8 9 0 .

ONE-HAND DEAF AND DUMB ALPHABET.

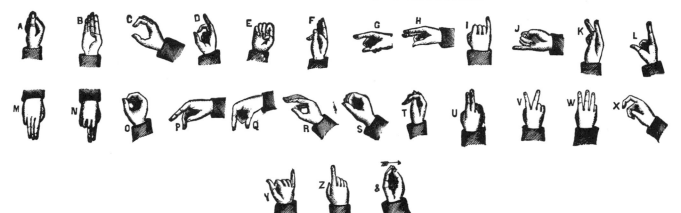

DORIC.

A B C D E F G H I J K L M N O P
Q R S T U V W X Y Z ?
a b c d e f g h i j k l m n o p q r s
t u v w x y z & $ 1 2 3 4 5 6 7 8 9 0 .

POINTED CONDENSED.

A B C D E F G H I J K L M N O P Q R S T
U V W X Y Z & $ 1 2 3 4 5 6 7 8 9 0 ? .

ELEMENTARE
TYPOGRAPHIE
MIT

ERBAR
GROTESK
SCHRIFTEN

DER
SCHRIFTGIESSEREI

LUDWIG & MAYER

FRANKFURT
AM MAIN

BEILAGE ZUR „GEBRAUCHSGRAPHIK"
ENTWURF, SATZ UND DRUCK
KÖLNER WERKSCHULEN
KLASSE ERBAR

Welche erfreuliche Veränderung zeigt sich schon seit zwei Jahrzehnten auf dem Gebiete der Schriftschneidekunst, gegenüber der Verflachung des Geschmackes in den letzten Jahrzehnten vorigen Jahrhunderts! Wir haben eine große Zahl von Antiquaschriften erhalten, die einen so hohen Grad der Durchgeistigung zeigen, daß sie den besten alten Vorbildern der Zeit des handwerklichen Schaffens an die Seite gestellt werden können.

Nur bei einer Schriftart, den Grotesk-Schriften, war seither von dem frischen Zug, der durch das Kunstgewerbe geht, nichts zu verspüren. Die Grotesk-Schriften hat man wohl in allen möglichen Breiten und Fetten gebracht, aber eine künstlerische Neugestaltung der Formen hat man unterlassen.

Man glaubte nach klassischen Vorbildern zu arbeiten und hat nur den Ungeschmack in eine verfeinerte Form gebracht, dadurch, daß man die langweilige Eintönigkeit noch peinlicher unterstrich.

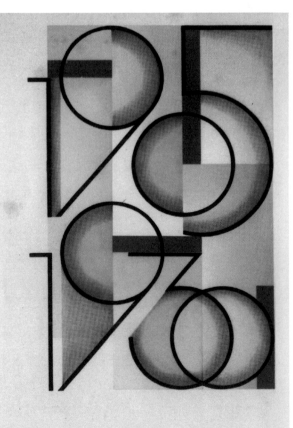

EIN VIERTEL
JAHRHUNDERT
DRUCKFARBEN
FABRIKEN
GEBR. HARTMANN
HALLE-AMMENDORF

ABCDE

FGHIJK

LMNOPQ

RSTUV

WXYZ

CAPTIONS

2 Advertisement for a reading lamp, photograph by Finsler, from *The Swiss Advertiser*, Germany, 1932. Courtesy Verlag Hermann Schmidt, Mainz

12 Cover of *Arts et Métiers Graphiques* (Deberny and Peignot, Paris, 1938). Redstone Press Collection

13 *Fregio Mecano* typeface from a typefounder's catalogue, Italy, c.1930. Courtesy Pentagram

14/15 From *Le Poème Électronique Le Corbusier* (Éditions de Minuit, France, 1958). Courtesy Lutz Becker

16 *Fregio Mecano* typeface from a typefounder's catalogue, Italy, c.1930. Courtesy Pentagram

17 Collage by Robert Michel, Germany, 1927. Merrill C. Berman Collection, New York

18 Top: designs for pictograms by Karl Peter Rohl, Germany, 1926. Bottom: logotypes, Germany, c.1940. Courtesy Verlag Hermann Schmidt, Mainz

19 Symbols from *Typogane*, typefounder's catalogue, Germany, c.1933. Courtesy Jan Solpera

20 *Condensed Grotesque* typeface with construction details and variants of single figures by Joost Schmidt, The Netherlands, 1926. Courtesy Richard Hollis

21 From *Le Témoin,* design by Paul Iribe, Paris, 1930s. Courtesy David Batterham

22 Cover of *Portfolio, No.3* designed by Alexey Brodovitch, USA, 1951

25/30 Pages from *Mise En Page: The Theory and Practice of Lay-out* by A. Tolmer (The Studio Ltd, London, 1932). Courtesy The Department of Typography and Graphic Communication at The University of Reading

33 From *Tabacchi Italiani Catalogo* (Italian State Monopoly, Italy, 1934). Courtesy David Batterham

34 Cover of the issue of *Campo Grafico* dedicated to Italian Futurism, design by Bona, Italy, 1939. Private collection.

35 Logotypes from various sources

36 Cover for *Sinopsis* by Miguel Prieto, Mexico, 1953. Courtesy Xavier Bermúdez

37/38 Typeface, mid-1900s. Private collection

39 Karel Sourek, cover for *Jazz* by E. F. Burian, Czechoslovakia, 1928. Redstone Press Collection

40 Page from *Arts et Métiers Graphiques* (Deberny and Peignot, Paris, 1930s). Courtesy David Batterham

41 *Bifur* alphabet by A. M. Cassandre, France, 1929. Courtesy Klingspoor Museum, Offenbach

42 From *The Lettering Manual* by Jan Sembera, Czechoslovakia, 1938. Redstone Press Collection

43 Cover of *Love Poems* by Otakar Storch-Marien, design by Josef Síma, Czechoslovakia, 1928

44 Page from a typefounder's catalogue. Redstone Press Collection

45 Cover of *Le Mot*, design by Paul Iribe, Paris, 1914. Courtesy David Batterham

46 Cover of *Divertissements Typographiques, Tome 1* (Deberny and Peignot, Paris, c.1935). Courtesy David Batterham

47 Symbols from a typefounder's catalogue, Italy, c.1952. Courtesy Pentagram

48 Typeface from a typefounder's manual, France, c.1940. Courtesy Verlag Hermann Schmidt, Mainz

49 Menu from *Arts et Métiers Graphiques* (Deberny and Peignot, Paris, 1930s). Redstone Press Collection

50 Top: wrapper for a joke ink-blot made of tin, Germany, c.1890. Redstone Press Collection. Bottom: from a typefounder's manual, USA, c.1900. Redstone Press Collection

51 Typeface from a typefounder's catalogue, USA, c.1955. Redstone Press Collection

52 From a children's alphabet, India, c.1980. Private collection

53 Top: lettering, design by K. C. Aryan, from *Calligraphy and Symbols*, India, 1966. Bottom: "Japanese-style" lettering. Courtesy Dover Publications

54 Alphabet design by Cehonin, Russia, 1925. Private collection

55 Book cover designed by Vialov, USSR, 1926

56 Poster for the opera *Casanova* by Jan Tschichold, Germany, 1920s, from *Gebrauchsgraphik*, 1928. Courtesy Gutenberg Museum, Mainz

57 Typeface designed for use on buildings by Edward Wright, UK, 1965. Courtesy The Department of Typography and Graphic Communication at The University of Reading

58 Specimens of wood letter from a typefounder's catalogue, UK, 1900

59 Cover of *Le Témoin,* France, 1934. Courtesy David Batterham

60 Specimens of embossing by Waterhouse Brothers and Layton Ltd. UK, 1890. Private collection

61 Page from a typefounder's catalogue, USA, c.1940

62 Film poster, India, c.1940. Nasreen Kabir Collection, Hyphen Films, London

63 Printer's symbols, India, c.1960

64 From "Lettres": Arts et Métiers Graphiques (Deberny and Peignot, Paris, 1948). Redstone Press Collection

65 Antique Olive typeface from a typefounder's manual, France, c.1940. Courtesy Verlag Hermann Schmidt, Mainz

66 Typeface from the album Schriften, Lettering, Ecritures, 1940s. Courtesy Klingspoor Museum, Offenbach

67 Photomontage by Paul Schuitema, The Netherlands, 1928. Courtesy Merrill C. Berman Collection, New York

68 Page from Hoffmann's Schriftatlas (Julius Hoffmann Verlag, Germany, 1930). Private collection

69 From a promotional folder for the Futura typeface, 1930s. Courtesy Klingspoor Museum, Offenbach

70 Typeface from the Signwriter's Manual of Typefaces by Richard Pípal, Czechoslovakia, 1956. Redstone Press Collection

71 Photograph by Jaromír Funke, Untitled, Czechoslovakia, c.1935

72 Logotypes for different types of insect repellent, Australia, 1950s

73 Printer's specimen page, UK, c.1910

74 Condensed wood letter typeface, USA, 1859

75 Illustration from Le Témoin, France, 1934

76 Theatre poster design by Vilmos Huszar, Berlin, 1931. Courtesy Merrill C. Berman Collection, New York

77 Symbols from Graphic News, Germany, 1939. Courtesy Verlag Hermann Schmidt, Mainz

78 Cover for BiF§ZF designed by Soffici, Italy, 1915

79 Cover for 7 dnei MKT (Seven Days at the Moscow Kamerny Theatre), design by V. & G. Sternberg, USSR, 1924

80 From the Signwriter's Manual of Typefaces by Richard Pípal, Czechoslovakia, 1956. Redstone Press Collection

81 Cover design for Dr. J. Branberger 1877 to 1927 (Akrostichon, Prague, 1927), design by Miroslav Ponc. Courtesy City Gallery, Prague

82 Top left: cover of Zlom by Konstantin Biebel, design by Karel Teige, Czechoslovakia, 1928. © Estate of Karel Teige. Private collection. Top right: cover of Diabolo by Vitezslav Nezval, design by H. V. Obrtel, Czechoslovakia, 1926. Private collection. Bottom: typographical compositions for Zlom by Karel Teige, Czechoslovakia, 1928. Private collection

83 Alphabet from Methods of Lettering by Fridrich Moravcik, Bratislava, 1975. Redstone Press Collection

84 Slipcase design for Art of the Present and Art of the Future by Murayama Tomoyoshi, Japan, 1924

85 Edward Wright, drawing for a typeface, UK, 1965. Courtesy The Department of Typography and Graphic Communication at The University of Reading

86 From a typefounder's catalogue, USA, c.1955. Private collection

87 Detail of "47 characters for easy learning" schoolroom poster, Japan, 1864. Private collection

88 From a printer's specimen book, USA, 1890. Courtesy Jan Tholenaar Collection, Amsterdam

89 From a signwriter's manual, UK, c.1900. Courtesy David Batterham

90 Page from Graphic News, Germany, 1933. Courtesy Verlag Hermann Schmidt, Mainz

91 Symbols from Trade Marks and Symbols (Graphis, Zurich, 1948)

92 Agency Gothic typeface, USA, c.1940

93 Cover of Le Mot, design by Paul Iribe, France, 1914. Courtesy David Batterham

94 Top left: cover for Shoka-Shinkei (Sensitivity of the early summer), design by Koishi Kiyoshi, Japan, 1933. Private collection. Top right: cover for Nonsense by V. Woodward (GIZ, USSR, 1927), design by B. Titov. Courtesy Misha Anikst. Bottom left: poster for the review Lacerba, Italy, 1914. Private collection. Bottom right: cover for Filmova' Dramata, screenplays by Louis Delluc (Ladislav Kuncír V Praza, Czechoslovakia, 1925). Private collection

95 Page from Hoffmann's Schriftatlas (Julius Hoffmann Verlag, Germany, 1930). Private collection

96 Front cover of Conversation with the Finance Inspector about Poetry by Vladimir Mayakovsky, design by Aleksandr Rodchenko, Russia, 1926. Courtesy Alexander Lavrentiev, The Rodchenko/Stepanova Archive, Moscow

99 Eye chart instruction cards for patients with hearing difficulties, (F. C. Cooper, London, mid-1900s)

100/106 Photographs and eye test charts from Eye and Instruments: Nineteenth-century ophthalmological instruments in the Netherlands by Isolde den Tonkelaar, Harold E. Henkes and Gijsbert K. van Leersum, 1996. Courtesy of BV Uitgeverij De Bataafsche Leeuw, Van Soeren and Co., Amsterdam

109 Advertisement from L'Architecture d'Aujourd'hui, No.10, France, c.1930

110 Renner Futura typeface from a typefounder's manual, Germany, c.1940. Courtesy Verlag Hermann Schmidt, Mainz

111 Economies of the world: Isotype chart by Gerd Arntz, 1930

112 Page from the Futurist theatre programme for Caffé Concerto, Italy, 1919. Courtesy Lutz Becker

113 Untitled alphabet by André Vlaanderen, Amsterdam, 1928. Private collection

114 *Les Catalanes*, a typeface design by Enric Crous-Vidal (never produced) from Caractère Noël, Spain, 1952. Courtesy Fundación Tipográfia Bauer, Barcelona

115 Back cover of *XXth Century* (English edition Christmas, 1938). Courtesy Brian Webb Collection

116 *Raleigh Gothic Condensed* typeface from a typefounder's catalogue, USA, c.1900

117 Friedrich Vordemberge-Gildewart designs. Top left/bottom left: covers for the architectural magazine *Forum*, The Netherlands, 1953 to 1951. Top right: prospectus for Kestner-Gesellschaft, Hanover, 1928. Bottom right: cover for advertising prospectus for the H. Osterwald Printing Works, Hanover, 1927, from *Vordemberge-Gildewart: The Complete Works,* Prestel Verlag. © The Vordemberge-Gildewart Foundation

118 Poster encouraging production, design by Dimitri Bulanov, USSR, 1928. Courtesy Merrill C. Berman Collection, New York

119 Stencil alphabet, USSR, c.1920

120 *Cinema* typeface from a typefounder's manual, UK, c.1950

121 Cover of *Gebrauchsgraphik,* Germany, 1928. Courtesy The Gutenberg Museum, Mainz

122 Cover of *Cobra Norato (Nheengatu du margem esquerda do Amazona)*, Brazil, 1931. Private collection

123 Hand-drawn typeface. Private collection

124 Logotypes from various sources. Redstone Press Collection

125 Cover of *Le Témoin,* France, 1935. Courtesy David Batterham

126 Alphabet, Hungary, c.1930. Jan de Jong Collection

127 From *Learn Artists*, drawing by A. Kruchenykh, Russia, 1917. Private collection

128 Version of *Patrona Grotesk* typeface, Czechoslovakia. Courtesy Jan Solpera

129 Poster encouraging production, design by Dimitri Bulanov, USSR, 1928. Courtesy Merrill C. Berman Collection, New York

130 Title page of *Zohna and Brides*, design by Ilya Zdanevich, USSR, c.1925. Courtesy Misha Anikst

131 Version of *Patrona Grotesk* typeface, Czechoslovakia. Courtesy Jan Solpera

132/133 Double-page spread from a typographic journal, Germany, c.1935. Courtesy Verlag Hermann Schmidt, Mainz

134/135 Typeface design by Alexey Brodovitch, from *Portfolio, No.1,* USA, 1950

136 Page from *Arts et Métiers Graphiques*, design by Roland Ansteau (Deberny and Peignot, Paris, 1930s). Redstone Press Collection

137 Page from the Marsh Stencil Machine Co. catalogue, USA, c.1947. Eric Finkel Collection

138 Page from a typefounder's catalogue, France, c.1900. Private collection.

139 Page from *Buffon Alphabet des Oiseaux*, (Pellerin and Cie, Paris, 1890). Courtesy Pentagram

140 Top: Piet Zwart, from *N. C. W. Catalogue*, The Netherlands, 1928. Merrill C. Berman Collection, New York. © DACS 2002. Bottom: Jan Tschichold, covers for the book *Fototek* nos. 1 and 2, Berlin, 1930. Merrill C. Berman Collection, New York

141 Graphic representation for the study of block lettering, Germany, c.1940. Courtesy Verlag Hermann Schmidt, Mainz

142 Top: Emmanuel Sougez, *Alfabeto* (Éditions Antonie Roché, Paris, 1932). Private collection. Bottom: Gaston Karquel, *Alfabeto fotogràfico*, text by Pauline David (Les Éditions du Compas, Paris, c.1935). Private collection

143 Trademarks from various sources. Redstone Press Collection

144 Top: front and back covers of schoolbook, India, c.1955. Private collection. Bottom: matchbox label, Japan, 1930. Redstone Press Collection

145 "Indian-style alphabet", UK. c.1940. Private collection

146 Art Nouveau alphabet from a signwriter's manual, France, c.1890. Courtesy Jan Tholenaar Collection, Amsterdam

147/148 Art Nouveau alphabet for signwriters from *Rotterdamsche Schilderschoole*, compiled by A. R. van der Burg, early 1900s. Courtesy Jan Tholenaar Collection, Amsterdam

149 From *Tabacchi Italiani Catalogo* published by the Italian State Monopoly, Italy, 1934. Courtesy David Batterham

150/151 Pages from *The Alphabetic Catalogue of the Place Names Belonging to the Nahuatl Language* by Antonio Penafiel, Mexico, 1885. Courtesy Pablo Butcher

152 *Egyptian No 2* typeface from a typefounder's manual, USA, 1872. Private collection

153 Back cover of *Le Témoin,* France, 1935. Courtesy David Batterham

154 Miguel Prieto, typography for book covers, a poster and a newspaper, Mexico, 1950s. Courtesy Xavier Bermúdez

155 Typeface designed by Enric Crous-Vidal, Spain. Courtesy Fundación Tipográfica Bauer, Barcelona

156 Cover design for the journal *Joaquim No. 15*, design by E. Di Vavalcanti, Brazil, 1947. Private collection

157 Hand-drawn typeface, source unknown

158 From *"Lettres": Arts et Métiers Graphiques* (Deberny and Peignot, Paris, 1948). Redstone Press Collection

159 Cover of *"Lettres": Arts et Métiers Graphiques*, (Deberny and Peignot, Paris, 1948). Redstone Press Collection

160 Covers for books by George Bernard Shaw, design by Ladislav Sutnar, Czechoslovakia, early 1930s. Courtesy Museum of Decorative Arts, Prague

163/172 Alphabet by Karel Teige, from *Abeceda* by Vitezslav Nezval, Czechoslovakia, 1926. © The Estate of Karel Teige

175 *Untitled* print with watercolour by Karel Teige, Czechoslovakia, 1927. Merrill C. Berman Collection, New York. © The Estate of Karel Teige

176 Horoscope from the article *Les Douze Maisons du Ciel* from *Verve*, France, 1938. Mel and Rhiannon Gooding Collection

177 Typefaces from a typefounder's catalogue, UK, c.1910. Redstone Press Collection

178 Logotypes from various sources.

179 Promotional brochure, design by Kozma, c.1930. Merrill C. Berman Collection, New York

180 Vassili Ermilov, *Constructivist composition*, USSR, 1923

181 Russian block alphabet. Courtesy David Hillman

182 Top: Bauhaus leaflet, design by Herbert Bayer, Germany, 1928. Courtesy Merrill C. Berman Collection, New York. Bottom: Typeface design by Herbert Bayer from *Offset, No.7*, Germany, 1926

183 Four covers for the journal *MA*, design by Lajos Kassak (Hungary), Vienna, 1920s. Private collection

184 Typefaces designed by Paul Carlyle and Guy Oring from *Letters and Lettering* (McGraw-Hill Book Co, USA, 1938). Courtesy Brian Webb Collection

185 Advertisement for Wurzburg Brothers (1930s) from *The Encyclopedia of the Packaging Industry* (Breskin and Charlton Publishing Corporation, New York, 1936). Courtesy Pentagram

186 Cover for *All Aboard for the Twentieth Century!*, design by Karel Teige, Czechoslovakia, 1928

187 Logotypes from *The Typeface Handbook* by E. Beaufort, Czechoslovakia c.1935. Courtesy Museum of Decorative Arts, Prague

188 Label found on bundle of newspapers, Japan, 1989. Redstone Press Collection

189 Ideogram with two birds, China, c.1700s. Courtesy Fang Chen

190 Top: cigarette pack designs (*Miss Mend* was the title of a popular series of detective novels), top right design by Aleksandr Rodchenko. Courtesy Misha Anikst. Bottom: poster advertising cigarettes. Courtesy Misha Anikst.

191 From a teaching manual for the study of Cyrillic lettering. c.1940. Courtesy Verlag Hermann Schmidt, Mainz

192 Cover for *Z Ponad* by Julian Przbos, design by Wladyslaw Strzeminski, Poland, 1930. Courtesy Merrill C. Berman Collection, New York

193 Preliminary drawing for the *Futura* typeface by Paul Renner, Germany, 1925. Private collection

194 *The Tippler* alphabet, USA, c.1940. Private collection

195 Page from a printer's specimen book, Germany, c.1930. Courtesy Verlag Hermann Schmidt, Mainz

196 *Egyptian* typeface reproduced in *Arts et Métiers Graphiques*, France, 1934. Redstone Press Collection

197 Project for a House of Advertising, from *Arts et Métiers Graphiques*, France, 1936. Courtesy Mel and Rhiannon Gooding

198 Printer's advertisement from *Gebrauchsgraphik*, Germany, 1930s

199 Alphabet design by William Dressler, c.1950, from *Lettering Art in Modern Use* (Reinhold Publishers, USA, 1952)

200 Film poster for Abel Gance's *Napoleon,* 1926, design by Jan Tschichold (photograph by Dominic Sweeney). Courtesy Royal College of Art Library

201 *Gothic Special* wood letters designed at the Hamilton Company, USA, c.1910, from *American Wood Type 1828 to 1900* by Rob Roy Kelly (Da Capo Press, USA, 1977)

202 Typeface with two styles, France. Private collection

203 Cover of *Le Mot,* design by Paul Iribe, France, 1915. Courtesy David Batterham

204 Publicity announcement for the *Futura* typeface "The type of our time", design by Paul Renner, reproduced in *Gebrauchsgraphik*, Germany, 1930. Courtesy Gutenberg Museum, Mainz

205 Logos from an Italian type manufacturer's catalogue, c.1950. Courtesy David Wakefield

206 Back cover of *Gebrauchsgraphik*, Germany, 1926. Courtesy Gutenberg Museum, Mainz

207 From a typefounder's catalogue, Germany, c.1935. Courtesy Verlag Hermann Schmidt, Mainz

208 Page from *Hoffmann's Schriftatlas*, (Julius Hoffmann Verlag, Germany, 1930). Private collection

209 Page from *Hoffmann's Schriftatlas*, (Julius Hoffmann Verlag, Germany, 1930). Private collection

210 Calligram by Guillaume Apollinaire from *SIC*, France, 1917

211 Top: Stencil typeface. Bottom: Advertisement from *Arts et Métiers Graphiques*, France, 1935. Redstone Press Collection

212 Page from a typefounder's catalogue, Germany, 1940. Courtesy Verlag Hermann Schmidt, Mainz

213 Page from *German Printing*, Germany, 1929. Courtesy Verlag Hermann Schmidt, Mainz

214 Top left: cover of *Integral*, Romania, 1925. Private collection. Top right: cover of *Blok*, Poland, 1926. Private collection. Bottom left: collage poster design by Mihailo S. Petrov for Zenit exhibition, Yugoslavia, 1924. Private collection. Bottom right: cover design by M. H. Maxy for *Contimporanul*, Romania, 1924. Private collection

215 Typeface from the *Signwriter's Manual of Typefaces*, by Richard Pípal, Czechoslovakia, 1956. Redstone Press Collection

216 Advertisement from *Arts et Métiers Graphiques*, France, 1931. Redstone Press Collection

217 Cover of *Le Mot* designed by Paul Iribe, France, 1915. Courtesy David Batterham

218 Sheet music cover, USSR, c.1910

219 Typeface, USSR, c.1905. Courtesy Pentagram

220 *Old Style Antique* from *Page's Wood Type Album*, USA, 1879

221 Designs by Diego Rivera, Mexico. Top: 1947. Bottom: 1950

222 Cover of *1946*, Mexico, June 1946

223/224 *Ludlow Gothic Extra Condensed* typeface, UK. Private collection

225 Title page of leaflets for *The Motley Square No. 2*, design by Max Burchartz, Germany, 1924. Courtesy Merrill C. Berman Collection, New York

226 Michel Leiris, *Amour,* cover of *Glossar: Where My Gloss Err,* France, 1939

229 Page from *The Sign Writer and Gloss Embosser*, UK, c.1890. Redstone Press Collection

230 Typeface design from the signwriter's manual *Modèles de Lettres sur des fonds differents*, France, early 1900s. Courtesy Collinge and Clark

231/232 Pages from *Petzendorfer, Schriften-Atlas,* Germany, 1894

233 Typeface design from the signwriter's manual *Modèles de Lettres sur des fonds differents*, France, early 1900s. Courtesy Collinge and Clark

234 Sheet from *Album for Signwriters,* The Netherlands, c.1900. Courtesy Jan Tholenaar Collection

235/236 Page from *Petzendorfer, Schriften-Atlas,* Germany, 1894

237/238 Typeface designs from *Modèles de Lettres pour peintres en bâtiments*, France, early 1900s. Courtesy Collinge and Clark

239/240 Pages from *Petzendorfer, Schriften-Atlas,* Germany, 1894

241 Sheet from *Album for Signwriters,* The Netherlands, c.1900. Courtesy Jan Tholenaar Collection

242 Typeface design from *Modèles de Lettres sur des fonds differents*, France, early 1900s. Courtesy Collinge and Clark

243/244 Pages from *Petzendorfer, Schriften-Atlas,* Germany, 1894

245 Typeface design from *Modèles de Lettres sur des fonds differents*, France, early 1900s. Courtesy Collinge and Clark

246 Sheet from the album *Decorative Signs*, France, c.1890. Courtesy Jan Tholenaar Collection

247/248 Pages from *Petzendorfer, Schriften-Atlas,* Germany, 1894

249 Convex lettering, source unknown

250 Typeface design from *Modèles de Lettres sur des fonds differents*, France, early 1900s. Courtesy Collinge and Clark

253 Cover of *Le Mot*, France, 1914. Courtesy David Batterham

254 *Condensed Grotesque* typeface with construction details and variants of single figures, Joost Schmidt, The Netherlands, 1926. Courtesy Richard Hollis

255 Poster for Florent pastilles, design by A. M. Cassandre (Hachard and Cie, Paris, 1930s). Private collection

256 Cover of *1946*, Mexico, May 1946. Redstone Press Collection

257 Gothic wood letters, UK, c.1837. Redstone Press Collection

258 Lottery poster, Portugal, 1989

259 Book cover design by J. Hesoun, Czechoslovakia, 1930. Private collection

260 Cover design for a printer's catalogue by Piet Zwart, The Netherlands, 1930

261 Catalogue design by Piet Zwart, The Netherlands, 1921. Brian Webb Collection

262 Lajos Kassak, *Typographic composition*, Hungary, 1921

263 Nikolai Suetin, sketches for shop signs, USSR, 1921

264 Page from *Typographic News*, Germany, 1926. Courtesy Verlag Hermann Schmidt, Mainz

265 Cover of *Gebrauchsgraphik*, Germany, 1924/25. Courtesy Gutenberg Museum, Mainz

266 Watercolour chart by I. V. Kliun from unpublished instructional volume, Moscow, 1942. ex. Costakis Collection

267 *Peignot* typeface, designed by A.M. Cassandre, France, 1937

268 Polish typeface. Jan de Jong Collection

269 Advertisement from *Arts et Métiers Graphiques* (Deberny and Peignot, Paris, 1930s). Private collection

270 Typeface designed by Vojtech Preissig, Czechoslovakia, 1914

271 Top: typeface from a signwriter's manual, Czechoslovakia, 1930s. Redstone Press Collection. Bottom: 'Three Jazz Reviews' poster, design by Frantisek Zelenka, Czechoslovakia, 1930. Courtesy Museum of Decorative Arts, Prague

272 Collage from *1946,* Mexico, 1946. Redstone Press Collection

273 Russian wood letter alphabet, USSR, c.1910. Courtesy Pentagram

274 *Didot* typeface specimen reproduced in *Arts et Métiers Graphiques,* France, 1930

275 Greek shop-signs and lettering. Courtesy Alan Fletcher

276 "Chinese- and Japanese-style" alphabets from *Alphabet Thesaurus* (Reinhold Publishers, USA, 1966). Private collection

277 Cover of *Mavo, No.3*, consisting of human hair, product labels and price tags, Japan, 1924. Private collection

278 Page from *Enciclopedia Practica Bompiani, Vol.1: La Cultura,* Italy, 1938. Courtesy Kit Grover

279 Specimen page from *The Book of American Types,* USA, 1941

280 Figure containing a complete alphabet from a book of parlour games, UK, c.1900

281 Cover of *Campo Grafico*, Italy, 1939

282 Typeface design by Morris Fuller Benton, USA, 1935. Private collection

283 Flourishes designed by Enric Crous-Vidal, Spain, 1953. Courtesy Fundación Tipográfica Bauer, Barcelona

284 Cover of *Gebrauchsgraphik,* Germany, 1930s. Courtesy Gutenberg Museum, Mainz

285 Logotypes from various sources. Redstone Press Collection

286 Russian alphabet probably based on *Bodoni*, Russia, c.1890. Private collection

287 Cover of *Art Journal,* USSR, 1923. Private collection

288 From *Tabacchi Italiani Catalogo* (Italian State Monopoly, Italy, 1934). Courtesy David Batterham

291 Mauricio Amster poster for *Cartilla Escolar Antifascista* (Ministry of Public Information, Madrid, 1937), "The Cultural Militias Fight Fascism by Combating Ignorance". Private collection

292/296 Pages from the *Antifascist Schoolbook*, design and montages by Mauricio Amster, photographs by José Val del Omar and José Calandin, Spain, 1937. Courtesy Lutz Becker

299 Cover of *d'Art Moderne,* France, 1932. Courtesy Alan Fletcher

300 Typographic composition, reproduced in *d'Art Moderne,* France, 1932. Courtesy Alan Fletcher

301 Cover of *Arts et Métiers Graphiques,* designed by Paul Iribe, France, 1932

302 Workers in the USSR: Isotype chart by Gerd Arntz, Germany, 1928

303 Page from typefounder's catalogue, Germany, c.1940. Courtesy Hermann Schmidt Verlag, Mainz

304 Typeface based on *Standard Light Extended*, Berthold Typefounders, early 1900s. Private collection

305 Page from *The First Six Books of the Elements of Euclid in which Coloured Diagrams and Symbols Are Used Instead of Letters for the Greater Ease of Learners* by Oliver Byrne and Charles Whittingham, UK, 1847. Redstone Press Collection

306 Okada Tatsuo, cover design for *Death Sentence,* Japan, 1925

307 Signwriter's alphabet, from the *Rotterdamsche Schilderschool*, compiled by A. R. van der Burg, The Netherlands, early 1900s. Courtesy Jan Tholenaar Collection, Amsterdam

308 A page of seals, Germany. Courtesy Museum of Decorative Arts, Prague

309 Page from a typefounder's catalogue, UK, c.1910

310 Top: from a promotional folder for the *Erbar* typeface, Ludwig and Mayer, Germany, 1930s. Courtesy Royal College of Art Library (photograph by Dominic Sweeney). Bottom: from a promotional folder for the printer Gebr. Hartmann, Germany, 1930. Redstone Press Collection

311 Photograph of printer-designers, from *Schriftenproben,* Germany, 1933

312 *Didot* typeface, France, c.1810. Private collection

313 From *Le Mot*, design by Paul Iribe, Paris, 1930s. Private collection

313/314 From *Le Poème Électronique Le Corbusier* (Éditions de Minuit, France, 1958). Courtesy Lutz Becker